Dream Big. Keep It Real. Get It Done!

THE POWER OF

PRAGMATIC PASSION

7 Common Sense Principles for
Achieving Personal & Professional Success

JOE BATTISTA
FATHER. COACH. MENTOR.

Foreword by New York Times Best Selling Author John U. Bacon

Praise for The Power of Pragmatic Passion

"Mr. Battista is genuine, enthusiastic, and credible. He listened to me and reassured me with his support and advice. I will continue to use the skills I've learned from The Power of Pragmatic Passion during college and when exploring careers."

Jamie B., recent High School Graduate

"Coach Battista has been a voice of reason and an inspiration for our daughter in assessing her future options. Through structured activities and with a great sense of humor, he has established a wonderful rapport with her, and he will continue to be a mentor in her life."

Wendy and Ken B., parents of Jamie B. (above)

"Joe's infectious energy and passion come through very clearly in The Power of Pragmatic Passion. His common sense approach provides a terrific road-map for adults of all ages to consider their path forward to success at any stage of their lives and careers. Given the remarkable success Joe has achieved by employing this approach throughout his career, and how well he translates that approach into this book, it is well worth reading and referring to Pragmatic Passion time and again."

Steve Kipp, Executive Coach, National Athletic and Professional Success Academy

"As an academic and psychologist, I'm fully aware of how we too often lose our grasp of useful, understandable, life-enhancing information in the maze of esoterica and other daily "noise." Coach Battista's Pragmatic Passion cuts to the core by offering a straightforward, clear, and yes — pragmatic approach -- to living a better life in all of its facets. Readers and audiences across age, education, and diversity spectra will find much value in Pragmatic Passion, and use it to pursue more productive lives into the future."

Dennis Heitzmann, Ph.D., Consulting Psychologist, Former Senior Director, Counseling and Psychological Services

"I met coach Battista after his keynote speech at my college sports banquet. His words and insight were very influential, and I will carry that newly gained knowledge with me throughout my life. His 1-on-1 coaching has been pivotal in helping me shape and achieve my academic and life goals. I'm grateful to Coach, and I believe everyone would benefit greatly from Pragmatic Passion."

Matteo Galieti, College Junior

"As I read The Power of Pragmatic Passion, it struck me that this book should be "required reading" for all people approaching (or early into) retirement. People who may have succeeded in life but are now asking "what's next?" People that have more to give to organizations, community, or society at large."

J. Alan Stewart, Retired, former Director of Land Development

"As a trusted coach and leader, this book captures Joe's approach to career and life using his 7 common-sense principles. This is a terrific resource for those seeking life and career insights, a motivating message, and a dose of Joe's humor!"

Cheryl Clark Bonner, Career Counselor and Co-Author of Your Career Planner

"Joe Battista forever changed my life. He is a kind person who cares deeply about helping others reach their potential. The Power of Pragmatic Passion offers practical, straightforward, and honest advice. This book is perfect for people who have a desire to learn and make a difference."

Brad Killmeyer, National Youth Speaker and Owner of Formulate Your Future

"Joe is one of the most inspirational leaders I've known. He creates breakthrough solutions that profoundly change existing paradigms. However, it's not "what" he does, it's "how" he does it that leaves a lasting impression."

Geoff Martha, Executive VP of Medtronic

The 7 Pragmatic Passion Principles

Dream Big. Keep It Real. Get It Done!

Whenever you are making critical decisions about your life and career you should ask yourself the following questions:

Purpose: Does it support my values, passions, and purpose?

Attitude: Will I have the proper attitude to commit to my goals and act on my purpose?

Sacrifice: Am I willing to make the sacrifices to persist and persevere along the way?

Servant Leadership: Does it serve others first and align with my servant leadership philosophy?

Inspiration: Will I be inspired to pursue my purpose with passion to "Get It Done?"

Options: Will I devote the time developing the best options so I make informed choices?

Nurture: Will it nurture me so I may live a joyful, fulfilling, passionate, and purposeful life?

Writing & Publishing Process by PlugAndPlayPublishing.com
Book Cover by Tracey Miller | TraceOfStyle.com
Illustrations and Logo by Malcolm McGaughy | McgDesign.net
Back Cover Headshot by Chuck Fong | FongStudio2.com
Edited by Lauren Cullumber

ISBN-13: 978-1724358271
ISBN-10: 1724358278

Disclaimer: This book contains opinions, ideas, experiences, and exercises. The purchaser and/or reader of these materials assumes all responsibility for the use of this information. Joe Battista and Publisher assume no responsibility and/or liability whatsoever for any purchaser and/or reader of these materials.

Dedication

It is with "The Attitude of Gratitude" that I dedicate this book to my mentors, teachers, coaches, friends, teammates, players, colleagues, my extended family, and especially my immediate family. Thanks for the life long love and inspiration from my parents, Joe "The Belly Man," and Angie "The Angel of my life," to the memory of my in-laws, Nellie and Francis "Smitty" Smith, to my brother Jan (who taught me all I know and half of what he knows) and his family, and to my children Brianna, Jonathon, and Ryan. I especially want to thank the love of my life, my wife, Heidi. She allowed me to "prolong adolescence" while I chased my hockey dreams for over 30 years. All have played a part in the forming of Pragmatic Passion (They just didn't know it!). I owe them all a debt I will never be able to fully repay.

My family (L to R): Jonathon, Joe, Heidi,
Brianna, and Ryan.

Table of Contents

Foreword

In the spring of 1986, I graduated from the University of Michigan and accepted a position as a faculty intern that fall at Culver Academies in Indiana. I taught two levels of U.S. history, supervised a dormitory, and coached soccer, hockey, and baseball – all for the princely sum of $9,000. That's right: high four figures. My honors history thesis was finally paying off!

I took Culver's offer over two much better salaries for one simple reason: Culver's legendary hockey coach, Al Clark. Ten years earlier he had started a team in the middle of Indiana's cornfields with an outdoor rink and a bunch of Hispanic kids enrolled in Culver's famed Black Horse Troop who had never skated before. Two years later, Culver won the first of dozens of state titles, and started attracting and developing world-class players. By the time Clark stepped down after four decades, he had sent more than 100 players to Division I college programs, and a half-dozen to the NHL, including 1986 NHL Rookie of the Year Gary Suter and current NHL Assistant Coach Kevin Dean.

It defied all logic, and everything I knew about the game. I decided I needed to learn from this man, so that's why I picked Culver. Clark became a lifelong friend and mentor, so by that measure, my unconventional decision was clearly the right one.

But I gained another great friend in the bargain: Joe Battista, the other assistant coach on Clark's staff. Joe is four years older, played the game in college, and simply knew more about it than I did, so I learned plenty from him, too – including passion. After a full day of teaching for me and counseling for him, followed by a fast-paced, two-hour practice, we'd still have the energy and desire to play full-ice one-on-one games against each other, which usually resulted in a few bruises because we were still wearing our coaching sweat suits. Our banged-up legs and arms are what passion looks like.

We even roomed together during our ten weekends on the road. Joe always came prepared – always. So prepared, in fact, that I learned to count on him bringing extra shampoo, soap, and toothpaste – and stopped bringing those things myself. On our many long trips to Madison, Chicago, Detroit, Toronto, Boston, and beyond, Battista would invariably have his nose in some grainy photocopied articles on the most picayune aspects of the game, including a ten-page treatise on how to defend a five-on-three powerplay.

Battista could not get enough, but his study of the game was highly systematic. The man had files of this stuff, and sought out anyone who could help him, right up to 1980 U.S. Olympic Coach Herb Brooks and his rival, "Badger" Bob Johnson, who once said, "Young Joe Battista! Great enthusiasm for the game!"

One day, when our year together was winding down, we were eating in the dining hall when he asked me what I wanted to do – on the assumption that my $9,000 position might not be my last one. I'd been thinking about that answer since my junior year in college, so I didn't flinch.

"I want to be a writer," I said.

Joe laughed. "But you haven't written anything. Good luck with that!"

I shrugged. I knew I had some work to do.

"Okay, smart guy," I said, "what do you want to do?"

He answered just as quickly as I had.

"Coach Penn State, go varsity, and build a new rink."

I returned the laugh. Joe's dream was crazier than mine.

"Guess you've got some work to do, too," I said.

Two years later I was writing by day and working in a restaurant by night. I had no idea what I was doing, but I kept doing it. I cranked out the pages, scribbled endless to-do lists, sought good mentors, overcame endless rejections, and stayed focused on my goal: I wanted to write books for a living, and the only way I knew to achieve that goal was through passion and perseverance.

After seven years of learning my craft and hacking away at the business, I finally got a great position writing Sunday sports features for The Detroit News – at age 31! After a great four-year run, I left to write books. I've now written ten critically acclaimed books, the last six national bestsellers.

But if Battista had written Pragmatic Passion thirty years ago, I would have saved a few years of toil and a lot of headaches! I had no clear philosophy, no particular approach, no specific systems for advancing my writing career. Unlike me, Battista strategically applied all those tools to his mission. And that's how he became Penn State's head hockey coach the year after we coached together, then rattled off 512 wins and six ACHA national titles in 19 seasons, while graduating over 90% of his players. Then he helped raise over $100 million to push the program to NCAA varsity status, and build a state-of-the-art, world-class ice arena.

Our paths were very different, but we remained close throughout. I helped him out by coaching at his hockey camps, and he helped me by hosting me for the 2012 Penn State football season, the subject of my book, *Fourth and Long: The Fight for the Soul of College Football*.

On October 11, 2013, I drove to Penn State to see the dedication game at Pegula Arena, and watch Battista participate in the ceremonial first puck drop.

Standing behind the plexiglass, I realized I was watching the realization of a crazy dream; one Joe had hatched a quarter-century earlier. He had done everything he said he was going to do – and then some. When he walked off the ice, I gave him a big hug, and we both got choked up.

Having watched Joe for 32 years now, I can tell you Battista practices everything he preaches: he dreams big, he keeps it real, and he gets it done.

If you want to achieve big dreams, Pragmatic Passion is how you do it.

Read on.

-John U. Bacon
New York Times Bestselling Author

A lifelong friendship with best-selling author John Bacon began with a shared passion for hockey. Joined here by fellow summer-camp instructors (L to R): Adam Brinker, Joe Battista, Clark Dexter, John Bacon, and Vincent Scalamogna.

Section One

Preparing for Passionate Performance

Read This First

"You don't have to be great to get started...
but you have to get started to be great!"

**Les Brown, Speaker and
Author of Live Your Dreams**

To get the most from this book, follow these two rules for success:

1. Pragmatic Passion Partner - Choose an adult such as a manager, teacher, coach, or parent as an accountability partner to assist in keeping you focused when reading this book. They must be candid and constructive, as well as supportive. They must challenge you to probe deeper by asking hard questions that may make you uncomfortable and even vulnerable. Your partner can assist as you build your "Pragmatic Passion Advisors Team" that will help you learn to apply the 7 Pragmatic Passion Principles to reach your goals.

Real Life 101

Here is a short list of people who have their own **accountability partner** in the form of a life or executive coach: Bill

Gates (Microsoft), Oprah Winfrey (Celebrity and Entrepreneur), Eric Schmidt (Google), Serena Williams (Tennis Star), Leonardo DiCaprio (Actor), and Meg Whitman (Chief Executive Officer of eBay).

"Your accountability partner keeps you on track and moving forward in all aspects" **Mike Staver, Author of Leadership Isn't For Cowards**

2. Digital Detox - To get the most from this experience; put your "digital distraction devices" away so you are not even tempted to peek at any social media during your reading time. **You must control your technology, so it does not control you.** Yes, I am serious. In her book *The Power of Off*, author Nancy Colier cites research that shows Millennials check their digital devices **150 times a day!** That is a lot of attention interrupted and focus lost! "Digital Detox" is a part of being focused and intentional. You can give yourself a 5-10 minute "technology break" only after one hour of focused reading. You must **earn** your break!

In an interview about his best-selling book, *Discover Your True North*, Bill George, former CEO of Medtronic, the world's leading medical technology company, noted: "As I walk through the library and the bookshelves of Barnes & Noble what I see are books for the CEOs and for the top echelon. But not everyone can make it to the top; there isn't enough room, anyway!"

> ## Important Pragmatic Passion Partner Information
>
> Remember that this journey is entirely about the person who asked you to be their mentor. I applaud you for accepting that honor. Keep in mind that this is about THEIR life. While you can provide resources and support, the best way to help is by helping them create, reveal, or cultivate their "Pragmatic Passion." Inspire them to read the book, do the activities, and hold them accountable to stay on a schedule. Give them the map, but let them decide the destinations and the routes, and be there to encourage them during their journey.

What I believe he is saying is that we need more assistance, resources, and **success coaching** for the rest of the people who can make their own significant contributions. For example, those from the middle class, from the inner city, and for the person who doesn't have the advantages of an Ivy League education.

This is not a textbook or an academic dissertation. It is purposely written with a blend of science and "Real Life 101" stories for those of us from that "middle" that desire to go from ordinary to extraordinary by using Pragmatic Passion.

It is my sincere hope that you are reading this book because you have big and bold dreams; because you want your life to have purpose; to be fulfilling, to be joyful; and because you are looking for guidance and assistance in making your personal and professional dreams come true.

Dream Big...Keep It Real...Get It Done!

Geoff Martha
Executive VP & President
Restoratives Therapies Group
Medtronic

Geoff Martha, Culver Academy graduate, former Penn
State Hockey Team Captain, and a member
of my Pragmatic Passion Advisors Team.
[*Photo by Rick Brandt*]

Introduction
What is Pragmatic Passion?
Dream BIG...Keep It Real...Get It done!

"Passion alone is not enough."

Greg Darley
Author of Passion Is Not Enough

Y OU are *unique*. You should pursue big, bold, passionate dreams...in a practical and pragmatic way. You can live a joyful, fulfilling life of value by pre-positioning yourself for success, and then getting into the action habit! The goal of this book is to help transform your life and career by applying The 7 Pragmatic Passion Principles.

"But everyone tells me to just follow my passions." Passion is most certainly essential for dreams to come true. But passion by itself is not sufficient. It must partner with a pragmatic, common sense approach and process, and be actionable to achieve personal and professional success. Pragmatic Passion is: developing great options, making informed decisions, and pursuing your purpose with passion!

You can be a high performer in your personal life and your professional life. You can discover and develop your real interests, cultivate your true passions, and identify your strengths and areas for personal and professional improvement. I want to assist by helping you to apply the **7 Pragmatic Passion Principles** in this book. These principles will help you to focus on pursuing your own path with your skill set, your desire, your passion, your cause, and your own unique purpose. It will both inspire you and motivate you to develop a success plan based on a pragmatic, common sense approach to help you develop your Pragmatic Passion!

You can begin this process at any time, regardless of your age or stage of life. Don't look back; it's in the past. Your future is ahead of you and it starts NOW! You just have to decide to begin and let me help you plan for your journey. This book will help you to develop your **Pragmatic Passion Success Plan**, which you will complete online upon finishing the book. Together we will help you find the courage to seek out solutions and put your ideas into action to avoid the "sea of sameness" and conventional wisdom, so you never become just another statistic in someone else's world.

Passion Point: I am one of the most passionate people you will ever meet. I believe that nothing worthwhile or transformational can be accomplished without great enthusiasm and passion.

So why then would I tell you that passion alone is not enough, and encourage you to be pragmatic in using your passion? Because my research, observations, and life experiences have proven to me over and over that passion, while essential, is not sufficient for you to reach your potential to achieve personal and professional success. Your passion must align with your purpose to allow you to actuate your plan to live a successful life based on YOUR definition of success.

Passion alone won't pay your bills or allow you to earn a living; or get you into the post-secondary college or vocational school of your choice; or help you become a high performing employee, executive, or entrepreneur; or allow you to live the life you ultimately desire. You cannot just blindly follow your passions without due diligence and proper planning. Identifying your passions is a process, and you can develop and cultivate your passions as you go along your life's journey.

"Life isn't about finding yourself. Life is about creating yourself." **George Bernard Shaw, Author**

Life is about exploring, creating, and learning to do something very well, to be passionate about what you do, so you have the time and money to pursue your hobbies and interests. Of course, the ideal situation is to get paid well for what you love to do! However, it usually takes time, it takes failing and learning, it takes effort to find opportunities, and it means placing yourself in a position to take advantage of good luck! I believe you will have a greater chance of success by aligning your passions with a purpose.

Pragmatic Point: Following your passion as a career only makes sense if it can also provide the financial rewards to allow you to pursue the quality of life you desire.

You may not possess some of the elite skills or natural talents that the highest performers in business, science, entertainment, or athletics possess. You know what? You can still become a high performer by developing your skills and being passionate while pursuing your purpose! It's ok to be unsure and uncertain and to try different paths. Provided you are willing to ask for help when prudent, to make the sacrifices needed to put your passion in motion, and to go after your dreams with confidence. This is your journey and you have to seek out the best resources to find your answers!

You see, I know this from personal experience.

Real Life 101: Developing Options and Making Informed Decisions

As a 10-year old growing up in a blue-collar family in the suburbs of Pittsburgh, I was introduced to the sport of hockey. What started as an interest quickly grew into a passion for me. I found myself reading everything I could get my hands on about the sport, skating every day possible, and playing street hockey relentlessly.

Passion Point: Hockey was exhilarating to me. I was mesmerized, obsessed, and couldn't get enough.

Growing up as an aspiring athlete in the "Steel City" meant that I had to try my hand at football and baseball, which was fun, but I was certainly not an elite talent, even if I thought I was in my mind. I was considered a versatile athlete who had a good work ethic and a competitive streak. Thankfully, I maintained good grades, especially in math and science. I had the guidance and influence of my mom and my closest friends and hockey teammates Lou Longo, Clark Dexter, and Don Studebaker to thank for that!

Pragmatic Point: Choose your friends wisely as they will have a tremendous influence on your life.

I loved the game and like many young kids, my dream was to get a college scholarship and eventually turn professional. When it was time for my 15-minute meeting with my guidance counselor in high school it went something like this: "Well Joe, you are strong in math and science, how about engineering?"

My immature and naïve response: "Sure, when do we drop the puck?" I really liked my counselor, he meant well, but in reality he had an impossible job. Counseling is sadly undervalued in public education.

Pragmatic Point: The average public high school has one guidance counselor for every 400 to 800 students!

So, I got out the Hockey News and looked at the top ranked college programs that also offered engineering and off I went very impractically visiting schools where I had absolutely no chance of playing varsity hockey, let alone on a scholarship. My parents did not have college degrees and we did not know who to turn to, or what questions to ask to find a good fit based on my interests, skills, and knowledge.

Pragmatic Point: I had the passion without the facts. I developed poor options and made an uninformed decision. I based my plan on incomplete information and unrealistic expectations.

After dealing with the realities of not getting a scholarship, I found myself at Penn State, essentially by accident, to study Nuclear Engineering. Why Penn State? Because my mother is a bright woman who, thankfully, recognized that I needed a Plan B. It offered in-state tuition, was far enough from home

Clark Dexter (L) and I (R) were the MVP's of the 1977 Dapper Dan All-Star Classic at the Pittsburgh Civic Arena. All my football and baseball friends were getting scholarships, surely Clark and I would be heavily recruited! Not exactly.

to feel like I went away for school, but close enough to get home if necessary. Why Nuclear Engineering? Because my mother worked for the Westinghouse Nuclear Division and like most kids, I chose a major where some family member or friend could hopefully get me a job!

I had no real passion for the major I had selected, but it sure sounded impressive at holiday family gatherings! I actually paid to play collegiate club hockey for the pure joy of the sport. Little did I know at the time, that it was my hands-on involvement as an officer with the club's Hockey Management Association, and the relationships with the people I met, that would play such an important role in shaping my future.

Pragmatic Point: Everyone needs a coach! Find the courage to ask for guidance from professionals.

After realizing I had made an uninformed decision with my major, I sought out the professional help of an academic counselor at Penn State. Jim Kelly helped change my life. He focused solely on helping me determine MY interests and passions. One of the tools he used in the process was the Jackson Personality Inventory Assessment. It came back with the following areas of interest based on my personality assessment:

1. Sales
2. Marketing
3. Physical Education Teacher

Say what? You couldn't get any farther away from a Nuclear Engineering degree. But it was not the assessment alone that set me on a different path. By asking me probing questions and focusing on my interests, the professional counselor quickly learned of my love of sports, especially hockey, and he gave me the best advice this 20-year old needed at that time. "You know that you can work in sports on the business side of the organization? Why not get a business degree? It aligns with your skills and interests."

Passion Point: That was an "A-ha!" moment for me. It created a pivot point for me based on real data and someone caring enough to help me discover my true interests and passion.

Earning a degree in marketing led to my first job after college, which was in, drum-roll please…sales and marketing! Better yet, it was with my very own hometown Pittsburgh Penguins of the NHL! I volunteered to coach the Junior Penguins as a hobby, but quickly discovered it was a true passion where I seemed to do well. I was 25 and single, so I decided it was pragmatic to pursue my coaching passion at that stage of my life. It was a rocky road for a few years, but the sacrifices paid off. At just 27, I would land an exciting, fun, and financially stable job at my alma mater in ice rink management, while also coaching Penn State's hockey team and being the director of their summer hockey camps. I did finally get to play in the N.H.L. (the Nittany Hockey League), the local recreational adult hockey league!

I loved what I was doing and belicved I was meant to coach young people. I also rekindled a friendship with a young lady I had met my junior year through the Hockey Management Association, and two years later we were married. I am blessed to be married to my best friend, Heidi, and to help raise our three children.

After 19 years of coaching, running hockey camps, and managing athletic facilities, an exciting new opportunity presented itself and I transitioned into athletic fundraising and administration. Hmmm, sounds a lot closer to sales, marketing, and a physical education teacher than a nuclear engineer! Most importantly, I had a fulfilling and passionate career.

So pragmatically speaking, I did what 99% of all athletes eventually do, and I became a *professional* in something other than playing my sport. By the way, the same could be said for many aspiring musicians, artists, dancers, writers, and architects, because passion is a necessary, but not sufficient, ingredient in becoming successful in such highly competitive fields. More later on using the vocation you have mastered to allow you to enjoy your true passions in conjunction with your career.

Is the time spent on our interests and passions in extracurricular activities such as music and sports wasted? NOT AT ALL! It is a means to an end that teaches sustainable and transferable life skills, such as: how to master a craft, how to be a part of a team, how to rebound from setbacks, and how to push yourself further than you thought possible. However, I do believe that far too many of us (including parents) have very unrealistic views on how difficult it is to become a pro-fessional musician, artist, actress, or pro athlete. We can spend an overwhelming amount of time and money chasing these highly improbable outcomes. If we used our resources more wisely, it could lead to improving skills and knowledge that are far more likely to set us up for personal and profes-sional success while also enjoying our passions (especially the ones that are really just hobbies). By all means, you can also continue to pursue getting paid for what you love to do as you develop more skills, knowledge, and gain experience. It's a process that takes time.

Do not misunderstand my point. A lot of good can come from the deliberate and intentional focus and skill develop-ment that is an outcome of time invested in these extracurric-ular activities. But there is an opportunity cost associated with an obsessive and unrealistic emotional and financial in-vestment that takes away from more pragmatic means for personal and professional growth. Think about the "starving artist" or the aspiring golfer who could be just as happy if they would find a vocation or job that allows them the time to pursue their passion (art, golf) as an avocation, a hobby.

Pragmatic Point: Unrealistically following passions in areas where we lack the necessary talents, skills, knowledge, deter-mination, and resources can lead not only to disappointment, but also low self-esteem, anxiety, and depression.

Research by Dr. Gabriele Oettingen, Professor of Psychology at New York University, warns of the dangers of simply us-ing "positive fantasizing" to dream about your future in her

2014 book, *Rethinking Positive Thinking: Inside the New Science of Motivation.*

> "While optimism can help us alleviate immediate suffering and persevere in challenging times, merely dreaming about the future actually makes people more frustrated and unhappy over the long term and less likely to achieve their goals. In fact, the pleasure we gain from positive fantasies allows us to fulfill our wishes virtually, sapping our energy to perform the hard work of meeting challenges and achieving goals in real life."

My own naïve dream of earning a college hockey scholarship and playing pro hockey gave way to a practical reality. But it was my *passion* for the game of hockey that led to a PURPOSE:

> To help young people discover the excitement and exhilaration of my sport by growing interest in the game of hockey across the country.

I am both happy and humbled to tell you that many of my dreams came true. Teaching hundreds of youth coaches and players as a USA Hockey Coaching Certification Instructor, coaching hundreds of players as an assistant coach and head coach, instructing thousands of kids at hockey camps and clinics, impacting many thousands more through the founding of the American Collegiate Hockey Association, and helping Penn State Hockey to build a new arena and reach varsity status with the generosity of Penn State alumnus Terry Pegula and his wife Kim.

It was by no means easy nor without its share of setbacks. It was a 35-year journey filled with ups and downs, highs and lows, successes followed by failures, followed by more successes. It took years of developing skills, accumulating experiences, overcoming adversities, putting mistakes behind me, and building real relationships and networks. It took a supportive family and courageous mentors, colleagues, and friends with a shared passion for my purpose. It was at times heartbreaking and painful, but it was rarely dull or boring. It has been an amazing, exhilarating, and fun ride that continues on for me!

Dreams do come true with a Pragmatic Passion
[*Courtesy of The Penn Stater Magazine*]

Dream Big. Keep It Real. Get It Done!

Over the years I have come to realize passion must partner with a pragmatic plan, and it must be put into action to achieve success. You must know yourself - your interests, desires, values, and skills, and the type of life you want to live in order to create a life plan. Your plan will change and evolve over the years due to internal and external factors, but you must start with a plan for a successful and fulfilling life.

By sharing real life lessons learned from mentors and colleagues, experiences from coaching, teaching, and managing thousands of students, athletes, campers, and employees, and by utilizing the years of existing research on this subject, we will work together to design your unique **Pragmatic Passion Success Plan**.

And that's exactly what we're going to cover in this book. I want to give you the tools and resources you need to figure all this out, and I will show you how you can intelligently and strategically choose what you want to do and achieve in your life and career by applying **Pragmatic Passion's 7 Core Principles**.

What is Pragmatic Passion?

According to the *Oxford English Dictionary*, being PRAGMATIC is "dealing with things sensibly and realistically in a way that is based on practical rather than theoretical considerations." Oxford also says that PASSION is having "an intense desire or enthusiasm for something."

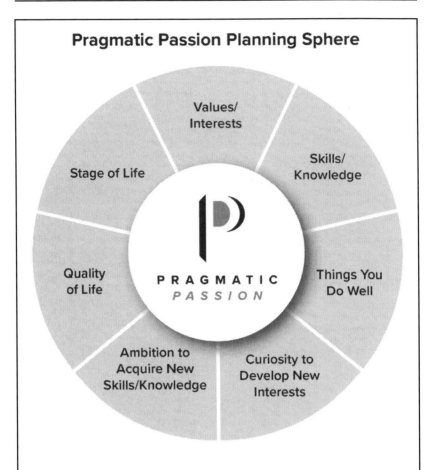

Pragmatic Passion Planning Sphere

Pragmatic Passion is the intersection of:

- Your current values and interests
- Your current skills and knowledge
- What you think you do well
- Your curiosity to develop new interests
- Your ambition to acquire new skills and knowledge
- Your desired quality of life
- Your stage of life

So, if we put them together, I see **Pragmatic Passion** as: Dream big. Keep it real. Get it done! It's the practical path to achieve success in your personal and professional life.

"Good intentions don't change the world. Ideas alone will change nothing. Desires don't feed the hungry. Ambition won't stop injustice. Enthusiasm alone will not reach the lost. Wishing changes nothing. To change the world, we must have more than passion." **Greg Darley, Author of Passion Is Not Enough**

Pragmatic Passion relies on the application of common sense principles before you make any critical or significant decisions. Always take an objective and dispassionate view of the issue to validate your conclusions. In essence, as my wife Heidi is fond of saying, "measure twice and cut once." Then cut away!

Part of your challenge is defining what a joyful, fulfilling, and successful life really looks like for YOU. This critical first step is often overlooked. But have no fear. In this book, you're going to work with your Pragmatic Passion Partner, your Pragmatic Passion Advisors Team, and this wise old hockey coach to help define what a successful life looks like for you by finding your own Pragmatic Passion and living life on YOUR terms!

By using a Pragmatic Passion philosophy, I honestly believe YOU can:

- Live a vibrant life

- Have a meaningful career (vocations)

- Enjoy interesting hobbies (avocations)

- Be passionate every day

- Contribute to the greater good

- Live comfortably with peace of mind

Why is Pragmatic Passion Important and Why Now?

- 70% of U.S. workers are not engaged at work (2017 Gallup Study)
- 13% of employees are actually passionate about their jobs (2017 Deloitte Insights Study)

Many employers think that can't possibly be true! Well, it is. And according to Jim Clifton, Chairman and CEO of Gallop Inc., "The American workforce has more than 100 million full-time employees. One-third of those employees are what Gallup calls engaged at work. They love their jobs and make their organization and America better every day. At the other end, 16% of employees are actively disengaged — they are miserable in the workplace and destroy what the most engaged employees build. **The remaining 51% of employees are not engaged — they're just there.**" How sad.

So, if that's the case, then we should be spending all our time simply finding our passion and a job that we love, right? Not so fast. **You still need to make a living!**

- 78% of Americans live paycheck to paycheck (2017 Harris Poll)

- 69% of Americans have less than $1,000 in savings (2016 GoBankingRates.com Survey)

- 56% of Americans have less than $10,000 saved for retirement (2016 *Money Magazine* study)

If we were giving out grades, the financial health of most Americans would receive a below-average score.

So, should we just quit our jobs, go back to college or vocational school to study what we love, and find a job that makes us more money? Chill! Just because you think you found a passion doesn't mean you should just blindly walk away from your current paycheck to take on more debt!

- 49% of American college students drop out before receiving their degrees (2015 Harvard Study)

- 33.4% of Americans have a College Degree from a 4-Year Institution (2016 U.S. Census)

- 1,120% is the amount college tuition and fees have increased since 1978 (Bloomberg)

- 42 million people owe $1.3 trillion in student debt (August 2016 *Consumer Reports* Magazine)

Clearly something is very wrong with our current way of thinking about life and career planning!

While the evidence is clear that those with college degrees, especially advanced degrees, earn significantly more on average than folks without degrees over the course of their careers, the process for planning has changed, given the dramatic increase in the cost of college. A "one size fits all" strategy for earning any level of college degrees (Associates, Bachelors, Masters, or Ph.D.) simply doesn't make sense. Incurring ridiculous amounts of debt for college, without a better understanding of your interests, values, passion, or purpose is not very pragmatic! This is especially true if the person doesn't currently have the maturity, determination, or financial resources, as many young adults don't. In Chapter 6, we will talk more about developing great options and making informed decisions based on YOUR skill set.

> **Passion Point:** Have the courage to set your own course and avoid being a statistic in someone else's world.

If you have the courage to forego the conventional wisdom by first discovering what matters most to you and what it will take to achieve it, then you will be way out ahead of those who blindly follow the flock. If you are willing to live a life driven by your passion for your purpose, you will avoid the trap that has snared so many of those who are so deep in college and credit card debt that they will struggle to live a joyful and fulfilling life with a comfortable retirement. Want a better plan for your life? Then read on!

Who Needs Pragmatic Passion?

Pragmatic Passion was designed for a variety of people in different stages of life. You need Pragmatic Passion:

- If you're looking for a new passion and purpose for your career or life

- If you're unsure of what you'd like to be when you grow up

- If you're a high school student (or their parent) and you are not sure if you're ready to go to college

- If you're a college student who suddenly realizes the subjects you are studying are not for you

- If you're a college graduate wanting a challenging first job that will lead to better jobs in the future

- If you're a go-getter and wish to learn new skills and move up within your company

- If you're frustrated with your current life situation and day-to-day routine and want to break free

- If you're a retiree who is looking for your next life challenge, whether it's full time or part time

...In other words, Pragmatic Passion is for all of us seeking direction, clarity, and a more focused purpose in life.

Pragmatic Passion was designed for a variety of people in different stages of life. Pragmatic Passion can help you create a success plan and help you get from point A to point B while avoiding the pitfalls most people fall victim to en route to a more fulfilling and joyful life.

"Find the sweet spot of something you are really good at, passionate about, and really enjoy doing." **Tal Ben Shahar, Harvard Professor**

How Does Pragmatic Passion Work?

In this book, we're going to cover the 7 Pragmatic Passion Principles. They are conveniently arranged to spell the word **P.A.S.S.I.O.N.** to help you remember them:

Purpose

Attitude

Sacrifice

Servant Leadership

Inspiration

Options

Nurture

Pragmatic Passion Success Sphere

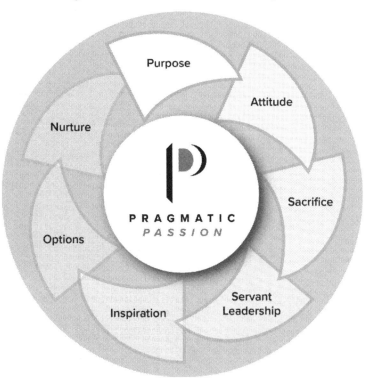

By applying the 7 Pragmatic Passion Principles in a step-by-step approach, you will learn:

1. To define what success looks like for you; to determine your values and interests; to help you reveal your passion and **PURPOSE**.

2. To choose your **ATTITUDE** toward everything in your life; to practice "Common Courtesy & Mutual Respect," and to have "The Attitude of Gratitude."

3. To use the "Power of Focus" and to learn to **SACRIFICE** by saying "No" so you can get to your "Yes." To practice persistence and perseverance, and to understand the difference.

4. To go above and beyond as a **SERVANT LEADER**; to use Civility, Humor, Empathy, Cooperation, and Kindness to resolve conflict. To be your best "you" as a leader, and to remember, someone has to care.

5. To find your **INSPIRATION** and surround yourself with people who make you better; to discover ways to positively motivate yourself daily; to be willing to push yourself beyond your current status.

6. To learn to develop outstanding **OPTIONS** and make informed choices; to set realistic, attainable, and purposeful goals; to design an organic, flexible, and purpose-driven life and career plan; to inspire you to act on your plans.

7. To **NUTURE** yourself and others; to be committed to professional and personal development; to be a life-long learner by developing a daily ritual to learn something new; to help make your dreams come true!

Are you ready to get started? Here's what I believe is necessary for you to discover your Pragmatic Passion:

First, you must believe in yourself. You're the only person who can change your life. Second, I encourage you to work with your Pragmatic Passion Partner to complete this book and the exercises and thought experiments inside. Third, you must have a growth mindset and be open-minded to both change and bettering yourself. Finally, you must make a commitment to *apply* what you learn in this book.

"Without application there is no true learning." **Chuck Kensinger, Facilitator, National Institute for School Leadership**

Regardless of your current circumstances you need a plan to realistically achieve your dreams. Let's go on a journey together to help you cultivate your purpose and to create goals that allow you to pursue that purpose with *passion*. Let's explore your Pragmatic Passion together.

Passion, Persistence, and Perseverance Matter. Stay Passionate!

Joe Battista
Pragmatic Passioneer

Overture

"Do not go where the path may lead, go instead where there is no path and leave a trail."

Ralph Waldo Emerson

You CAN achieve your personal and professional dreams. You can live a joyful, happy, meaningful life that aligns with your purpose. This is best accomplished only *after* you begin to discover and determine your values, cultivate your true passions, and define your purpose in a systematic way by developing a plan that is organic and grows along with you. How do you do this?

1. Use Common Sense. Using the 7 Pragmatic Passion Principles, which have a strong foundation of common sense, you will have a higher probability to succeed. I believe you can find the willpower, energy, and the discipline within you to make it all come together by using this common sense approach to setting goals and planning for a successful life.

2. Embrace Change! Change always has been, and always will be a constant in the world and the sooner you accept this, the more confident you will become in handling change. Your passions will change as you mature and gain new skills, knowledge, and wisdom during your journey. Accept this now: Embrace the changes that will occur in you in order to grow into the best version of you! Change is the "stuff of life" and helps turn your journey into an exciting adventure.

"But change is frightening, uncertain, and could lead to embarrassment. I am not sure I can do this."

Yes you can!! You just need some guidance and coaching to get you started and help keep you on track.

Through this book, you can lean on my years of real life experience working with students, their parents, managers, executives, and business owners, as a coach, instructor, administrator, and mentor, to be a guide and a resource.

3. Conquer your fear. We all make mistakes and are all flawed in some ways as we constantly search for answers. So what! It just means we are human. I have made more mistakes in my life than I care to admit (including a few big ones). Try to learn from those mistakes and put them behind you. The biggest mistake in life is being afraid to make one! Learn to practice forgiveness and be willing to receive it from others.

"Great spirits have always encountered violent opposition from mediocre minds." **Albert Einstein**

Despite setbacks and disappointments, there have been far more blessings bestowed upon my family and me. I have such an attitude of gratitude for the life I have led so far and owe much of what I have experienced to the guidance of others: family, friends, teachers, coaches, colleagues, teammates, mentors, and my faith.

Notice I didn't say anywhere that I was really smart, nor did I come from money. I don't have an Ivy League education or a Ph.D. (unless you count my <u>P</u>enn <u>H</u>ills <u>D</u>egree!).

I am a "Passioneer," to use a term from friend Steven Mezzacappa, the founder of "Passion with Purpose." I genuinely want to help YOU explore and develop a purpose and a direction in your career and life. I believe I am an innovator and a change agent in an ever-changing world and my new goal, my Pragmatic Passion, is to help you and others to live joyful, fulfilling, and purposeful lives.

"To keep our passion alive, we must constantly fuel our souls with the things that inspire our mind, empower our will, and encourage our emotions." **Steven Mezzacappa, Passioneer and Founder of "Passion with Purpose"**

We live in a marvelous time where innovation and technology have created possibilities never before seen and we are interconnected with the world and each other like never before.

Yes, this also creates challenges, but I believe that by using Pragmatic Passion, you will be in a better position to benefit from and enjoy all this innovation - and to use it to make a positive difference in our world.

Passion, Persistence, and Perseverance Matter

Pragmatic Point: Showing up every day and grinding it out, even on those days when you're low on passion fuel, is what separates achievers from fantasizers.

Take a moment and look closely at the Pragmatic Passion logo and describe what you see?

You should see two very different "P's." First is the outer, more structured "P." It represents the Pragmatic part of your brain, i.e. your common sense. The second "P" may be a little harder to see as it is less structured, not fully formed, and represents your Passion. You get bonus points if you also see the "D" representing Disciplined Determination. For without disciplined determination, dreams are highly unlikely to come true! My experiences have led me to this formula for success: Develop pragmatic plans, based on a purposeful passion, and put your plans into action with disciplined determination.

Pragmatic Plans

+ Purposeful Passion

+ Disciplined Determination

= SUCCESS

In order to achieve self-improvement you must be willing to learn, break through old barriers, and not worry about critics and naysayers. To win the game, you must be completely engaged in the game. You must be "in the arena."

Passion Point: In the arena of life, it is not the critic who counts. Have the courage to try your best!

One of the most inspiring speeches ever given was, "The Man in the Arena," by President Theodore Roosevelt on April 23, 1910. This speech is framed in my office where I see it every day. It is a reminder to have the courage to try things to the best of your ability and ignore the critics.

The message is especially relevant in today's social media driven world where we are inundated with "fake news." We are surrounded by "critics without credentials," those anonymous Internet commenters who criticize just for the sake of being contrary and negative because *they* have no real passion or purpose of their own.

I have taken the liberty of modernizing "Teddy's" speech below:

> "**It is not the critic who counts**; not the **person** who points out how strong **people** stumble, or where the doer of deeds could have done them better. The credit belongs

to the **person** who is actually in the arena, whose face is marred by dust and sweat and blood; who strives valiantly; who errs, who comes short again and again, because there is no effort without error and shortcoming; but who does actually strive to do the deeds; who knows great enthusiasms, the great devotions; who spends **themself** in a worthy cause; who at the best knows in the end the triumph of high achievement, and who at the worst, if **they** fail, at least fail while daring greatly, **so that their place shall never be with those cold and timid souls who neither know victory nor defeat.**"

I believe what "Teddy" was saying is that it is far better to have the courage to try your best and fall short, than to have never tried at all. When you are engaged in a worthy cause and someone is trying to tear you down, ridicule you, or create a barrier for you, simply look at it as a compliment and a source of motivation.

These critics and naysayers haven't taken the chance, put their reputation on the line, or had the guts to go after their dream. But you **do** have the guts to go after your dream. Bring it on!

"Kids were laughing in my classes, while I was scheming for the masses. Who do you think you are, dreaming 'bout being a big star?" **Dan Reynolds, Imagine Dragons. "Thunder." Evolve**

Just Say No to Excusitis!

What is Excusitis? A common ailment when people use all kinds of excuses to justify their poor performance or a lack of action.

So if you have a dream but keep on making excuses and thinking negatively, such as telling yourself: "I am not smart enough," or "I don't have incredible physical, artistic, musical, or athletic skills," or "I have made some incredibly bad decisions and am afraid of being embarrassed again," or "I have failed more times than I care to admit." SO WHAT! Again, this just proves you are human. I assure you that every person in the history of the world has had times of doubt. So, forgive yourself, dust yourself off, and move on.

If you feel like the odds are against you, if you feel that your dream is impossible, if you have a dream, but feel that no matter how hard you try, nothing good ever happens, then you are just like most people (including me). SO WHAT! Again, you are human. Your experiences become wisdom for your future. **Move on!**

Pragmatic Passion will help you understand that you DO have the confidence and the courage within you to pursue your dreams, regardless of the critics. The only critic you need to care about is the one staring back at you from the mirror. That person believes in you!

"Mistakes are just temporary setbacks. Regroup, persevere, and move on!" **Joe Battista**

Do not be afraid to make mistakes. They will happen. Do not let a setback or a current lack of confidence paralyze you and keep you out of the game of life. High achievers, and those who are truly at peace in their life, know that you must embrace mistakes as opportunities to learn. No success is forever and no mistake is fatal unless you give up. **Grind on!**

So now that we have gotten the "excusitis" out of the way, it's time to dive deep, challenge yourself, and put Pragmatic Passion to work for you. Improve your odds of being successful by applying the 7 Pragmatic Passion Principles with the help of your Pragmatic Passion Partner!

It takes more than a dream. It takes more than passion. It even takes more than a plan. It takes ACTION! Let Pragmatic Passion prepare you for success "in the arena" of life. Let's do this!

Section Two

Dreams into Goals into Reality

Chapter 1
Purpose

"The two most important days in your life are the day you were born and the day you find out why."

Mark Twain, Legendary American Author

Chapter 1 Objectives:

1. To go from self-discovery to self-realization

2. To define what success looks like for you

3. To help you determine your values and interests

4. To help you develop your passion and purpose

5. To write your Pragmatic Passion Personal Vision Statement

"Your dreams have a much greater chance of coming true when you have a purpose." **Joe Battista**

We all need a starting point and taking that first step is critical. Over the course of your journey you will need to make adjustments and to pivot occasionally. But common sense tells us that you are more likely to achieve the life you want if you have given it intentional thought and developed a plan to get you started.

This chapter will end with you creating your own **Pragmatic Passion Personal Vision Statement.**

Objective 1: Self-Discovery to Self-Realization

"While we are obsessed with the pursuit of personal happiness, it is the understanding of your meaning in life that is the secret to your resilience and success." **Emily Esfahani Smith, Psychology Instructor, University of Pennsylvania**

The research for this book included watching hundreds of TED Talks, Goalcasts, YouTube videos, listening to audiobooks and podcasts, reading new books, and interviewing experts in a variety of fields. It included looking back on my own life experiences and combining what I have observed with what I have learned. I probed deeper into my own belief systems and philosophies to understand my own values and how they set me on my path. Now it is time to share it with you.

All of this research has either validated my beliefs or challenged me to consider new ideas. It's been invigorating and enlightening. It has made me realize that my own purpose is to serve others by helping them to discover their own Pragmatic Passions. It's also given me the confidence to push forward with this concept because I believe deeply that if we explore and discover our passions and purpose, we will live a more joyful and fulfilling life. Most people simply don't spend enough time and energy on this most important aspect of self-discovery and life planning.

In his 2013 YouTube talk at Google, Robert Greene, author and lecturer, discusses his book *Mastery*. I focused on his description of the process of Mastery in which he says this:

> "This process begins with **the critical first step** of choosing which field of study or subject to pursue. Creative people are those who opt for career paths that mesh with their deepest interests and inclinations. ...Feeling personally engaged and motivated in their work, they focus more, they learn faster, they are more patient and more persistent than other people."

I want to emphasize "the critical first step" because this is where I believe most people falter and do not spend enough focused time. Long before you can become a master at something, you need to explore and discover what that "something" might be. That is where I believe Pragmatic Passion can help you.

You will work with your Pragmatic Passion Partner to review your answers in the categories below in order to prepare to form your Pragmatic Passion Personal Vision Statement at the end of this chapter:

- Values & Interests
- Skills & Knowledge

- Natural Talents/What You Think You Do Well / What Others Say You Do Well

- Areas for Improvement/Passion Pitfalls

- Passions and Causes

- Desired Quality of Life/Stage of life

"If you want to be successful, you need to think of yourself as a personal brand. A personal vision statement is a critical piece of your brand because it helps you stay focused." **William Arruda, Author, Ditch, Dare, Do**

Have you ever really spent focused and deliberate time exploring ways to discover or create your Passion and Purpose? Has anyone ever coached you through a process to ask the really deep questions that can help you to reveal the components for your life and success plan? If you answered yes, when was the last time you had a check-up? Cars get inspected; they get oil changes, and tires rotated. Do the same for your life plans!

When have you actually looked in the mirror and asked yourself the tough questions that will help you create the life you truly desire? This will only work if you give deep thought and reflection on the things that matter most to you in life. Once you do a deep-dive into your heart, you begin to have clarity for your life.

"The Mirror doesn't lie, so don't try to fool it." **Jeffrey Hayzlett, Best Selling Author of The Mirror Test: Is Your Business Really Breathing and Think Big, Act Bigger: The Rewards of Being Relentless**

It's YOUR life. Take *charge* of it!

In this chapter, we'll also explore what success looks like for you and how to live a purposeful life that makes a difference to others. Finding your purpose (or cause) is a blending of art and science, which is why you need to utilize assessment tests, your own intuition, guidance from your Pragmatic Passion Partner, and the input from a professional counselor as well. You will discover that it requires discipline, focus, persistence, and perseverance to pursue your passions and your purpose.

Have you heard any of these phrases?

- "You can be anything you want to be."
- "Just follow your passion and dreams."
- "Do what you love and the money will follow."

If it were that easy, don't you think everyone would do it?

This advice tends to come from well-intentioned parents, relatives, friends, co-workers, motivational speakers, and even some well-meaning guidance counselors. But can you realistically be *anything* you want to be? Can you simply *just* follow your passion and dreams and watch them all come true? Will the money *really* follow simply because you do what you love?

While these folks have good intentions, most don't really know anything about your skill set and they have a limited idea of what it would take for your specific dreams to come true. They are not being dispassionate or objective in evaluating you because they don't want to hurt your feelings. I have witnessed this play out too many times when people simply set themselves up with unrealistic expectations without taking the time necessary to really research their interests, skills, and abilities to see if they align with their dreams. They either don't understand the price that must be paid in sacrifice and hard work to achieve their goals, or they are not willing to persevere when the going gets tough.

Chess aficionado Dr. Eugene Furman, a materials science researcher by trade, passed along this takeaway from a chat he had with chess Grandmaster Semon "Sam" Palatnik. Dr. Furman's interpretation: "You can be a *good* engineer and make a good living. You can't just be a *good* chess player and make a living playing chess." That can be said for a lot of high profile jobs in sports, music, theatre, etc. To make a living at these highly competitive occupations, you must be a master of your craft.

"There is a price for everything. Goodness is free, but greatness will cost you. The questions is, are you ready to pay the price?" **Delatorro McNeal II, Author of Caught Between a Dream and a Job**

I am not simply being a cold, harsh realist by saying this. The lesson to learn was that I was never going to be a brain surgeon or the CEO of a major corporation simply because I wanted to be. I was not going to become a professional hockey player simply because it was my dream. Just because I loved sports, didn't mean I was going to have a career in the industry.

Dream big. Keep it real. Get it done. I have seen enough people set themselves (or worse, their kids) up for failure for chasing after unrealistic dreams without the facts, because just like me, they developed **poor options** and made **uninformed decisions**. Just like the younger version of me, they based a plan on the wrong information and unrealistic expectations.

So, let's look at **modified** versions of the well-wisher's phrases:

- "You can be anything you want to be...*if you have the talent, aptitude, and work ethic to acquire the necessary skills and knowledge.*"

- "Just follow your passion and dreams...*to inspire you to learn the skills in the right industry to be successful.*"

- "Do what you love...*become an expert at your craft*...and the money will follow."

Your dreams can be big, ambitious, and even audacious. But they must also be attainable from a practical perspective, as they are very dependent on your skills and knowledge, your willingness to continue developing your skills and knowledge, your daily discipline, and your determination.

Pragmatic Point: Become so good at your "something" that you love what you do. Simultaneously keep exploring opportunities that will continue to help you discover your purpose and then put your heart and soul into pursuing that purpose with passion.

As we know from the statistics on page 28-29, in our desire to find the "perfect job," the harsh reality is that most Americans do not feel interested in or engaged at their jobs. They may have wrongly believed their passion could be one and the same with their career, or vocation, when in reality their passion was really more of a hobby, an avocation, with no economic benefit. In essence, it couldn't pay the bills.

Your interests can be documented, new skills can be learned, your attitude developed, and your passions and purpose discovered and cultivated. You need a system that holds you **accountable**. You need a mentor, a coach, or a trainer. If you think you can do it yourself then go for it! But if you start to lose momentum or interest, then you need to be smart enough and have the courage to reach out for assistance. Even if you must seek professional assistance, it will be worth the time and money.

"But I don't have the time or the money."

I am calling "bull" on that because you can take five minutes right now and come up with a list of all the time and money you waste on useless things that do not improve your quality of life. Remember that Pragmatic Passion is the cure for "excusitis." It's not that you don't have the time or money. It's the fact that you haven't made this a top priority in your life yet. Because when you actually do make creating, cultivating, and discovering your purpose a top priority, you will find the resources you need to make things happen. Pragmatic Passion starts with having a realistic evaluation of your current values and interests, and determining if they are compatible with your skills and knowledge.

Pragmatic Point: While I am a Passioneer, I am a firm believer that your dreams must be based in reality.

I have learned that "perfect can be the enemy of great" and that "feedback is a blessing" and the best lessons learned are often the toughest to admit. Have the courage to seek out and listen to the candid and constructive "corrections" from your Pragmatic Passion Partner and additional members of your inner circle that are necessary to create real change in you.

Consider this analogy. When you are ill, you visit a medical doctor to determine the type and severity of the illness. What does the doctor do? They take your vital signs, ask you a series of questions, and administer tests to determine what ails you. Sometimes the doctor quickly knows the diagnosis, prescribes your next steps, and your visit is short and sweet. Other cases are much more involved and require a process of elimination to discern the illness and possible causes, which may take a long time to determine. Different treatments are then attempted, especially if the illness is serious, before finding the right solution.

Now suppose instead you are going to see the "purpose" doctor. The doctor would begin essentially the same way. They want to know about your background and experiences, will ask you about your values, interests, and passions, and they will administer a series of assessments to determine a direction. You must think of this discovery of your passions and purpose in the same way. For some it is a simple process and they know from an early age about their passions and purpose. For others it is a long process of trial and error.

Why do you so easily seek professional assistance for an ailment, but you won't ask for professional assistance to help you create and determine your true passions and life's purpose?

"On the road to success, there are no shortcuts." **Anonymous**

There are no shortcuts to success. No one owes you anything. You don't deserve anything unless you have earned it! The "entitlement" attitude that pervades this world is going to catch up with us sooner or later. There are those who believe they can simply follow their passion, do what they love, do it for the least amount of effort, and somehow get paid a lot of money, so they can live a life of luxury with little or no stress. Sorry, but without amazing natural talent, a big inheritance, or an improbable stroke of luck, this lifestyle is highly unlikely.

What if I was passionate about surfing the Internet in the morning, golfing in the afternoon, and going out to parties every night? How easy do you think it would be to find someone to pay me to pursue those passions? While that sounds great, it doesn't seem very pragmatic or realistic.

There are people who fantasize about a carefree, financially independent life (without sacrifices), but it almost always remains just a dream. Just like winning the lottery, it's highly unlikely. Some claim to have no interests, no passions, and no purpose and are content to live off of others. There is no honor in taking advantage of others while lying on the couch doing nothing. I say shame on them!

Pragmatic Point: This book is *not* a career-planning guide. There are plenty of resources out there for you to explore and private career services counselors to assist with the nuts and bolts. This book is meant to serve as a guide for helping you achieve personal and professional success through the application of the 7 Pragmatic Passion Principles. Visit www.PragmaticPassion.com/bookresources for recommendations on more career planning resources.

Objective 2: It Starts By Defining Success For YOU!

"Begin with the end in mind." **Dr. Stephen Covey, Author of The Seven Habits of Highly Effective People**

YOU must decide what matters to YOU and how you define YOUR success. Are you searching for happiness, fame and fortune, contentment, adventure, financial freedom, a balanced life? Can you really achieve *all* of these goals?

Perhaps you can, as long as you don't expect all of them every single day! This life is a journey and there will be wonderful, joyous times and difficult, challenging times. Figure out what matters to you and do your best to make each day a great one, as often as possible. The ancient Greeks sought *Arête*: the perfect blending of body, mind, and spirit. There is a sign just outside the fitness room at my local gym that states: "True wealth is a balance of spirit, mind, and body."

For every public success story like a Bill Gates, Oprah Winfrey, Michael Jordan, Elon Musk, Jeff Bezos, Serena Williams, Mark Zuckerberg, Ellen DeGeneres, or Steve Jobs, there are millions of people who have reached their own level of success as they have defined it. They are living fulfilling, joyful, and successful lives in their own right. Perhaps with a lot less stress, as well! Keep in mind that some of the wealthiest and most celebrated people in history have also lived some of the most tragic private lives. Don't focus on what society thinks of as successful. You focus on YOU!

"You can do anything you want...you just can't do everything you want!" **Michael Hyatt, Founder of Intentional Leadership**

What are your values and core beliefs? What inspires you? What makes you want to leap out of bed every morning with enthusiasm? What kind of a life do you want to live? What difference do you want to make in the world?

It may seem daunting and a bit stressful asking you to think about such deep questions, but here is the good news: this is part of a process and just a snapshot of where you are today. There will be times of self-doubt, fear, pain, frustration, and even anger. But with proper time, the right attitude, intentional learning, focused practice, and natural maturity, your definition of success will become clearer to you. You will learn by exploring, discovering, and experiencing life.

There will be many attempts, followed by failures, followed by adjustments but as long as you learn from these experiences there will be progress. There may even be an "A-ha!" moment (or multiple moments) in your lifetime.

Give the following exercises in this book your best shot and after you have completed them, review each section with your Pragmatic Passion Partner.

Here are a few tools to help clarify what matters to you in life, to assist you in determining how to define success for you, and to assist in your self-awareness process.

1. Vision

"Vision precedes purpose, fuels hard work, and yields success." **Lara Tabet, Middle East Business Developer, Brand Ambassador, and Philanthropist**

A lot of people talk about vision as a guiding force for decision-making. Corporations have vision statements. People have personal vision statements. I emphatically believe that they are needed. But how do you create one? Well, it might be easier than you think. I have been teaching athletes to visualize for over 35 years. For those who embrace it, I believe it makes a big difference. So give it a try!

Start by daydreaming a bit. Yes, I am actually telling you to do a little daydreaming, just in a more pragmatic, intentional way. Envision the life you wish to live by using your imagination. Make a movie in your mind's eye from your perspective about your life. Try to be as specific as you can be, but not just about the outcomes – make it about the journey. Use this "mental rehearsal" to see yourself making the sacrifices and overcoming obstacles, because there will be adversity in your journey. Visualize yourself achieving goals and milestones and grinding it out on the path to achieving your dreams. After all, if you are going to make a personal documentary, you may as well make it award winning!

For more on Visualization Techniques go to:
www.PragmaticPassion.com/bookresources

You must find a place of peace and quiet and set aside the time needed to be deliberate and intentional in your focus. This is known as mindfulness. You may choose to have relaxed but energized instrumental music in the background, but it is best to do this without any distractions. This is also a time for a Digital Detox! Now, close your eyes and take a deep breath through your nose and slowly release your breath through your mouth for an eight-count. Relax and feel the confidence flowing through you. Visualize yourself learning new skills, pushing past old benchmarks, and achieving the goals you set. See yourself living a purposeful and fulfilling life!

Take as much time as you need. Once you have visualized your ideal life, write out a page or two of what your "movie" looked like. There is no right or wrong answer here. Your story is YOUR story, and it should be deeply personal to you alone and only shared with your Pragmatic Passion Partner.

Based on YOUR Movie:

- What does the ideal "YOU" look like today?

- What does the ideal "YOU" look like 3-5 years from now?

- What are your biggest fears that are preventing your dream from happening?

- What does a "big achievement" look like to you?

- What is the greatest adversity you might face?

- What is the greatest obstacle you will overcome?

- Define success for YOU.

Pragmatic Point: Put this in your calendar right now. Do a semi-annual "Pragmatic Passion Vision Check-up" to be sure your "documentary" is updated to reflect your new skills, knowledge, and experiences.

Keep these answers handy, as you will re-do them (perhaps several times) when you have completed this book. Hopefully, you will create new ones throughout your life's journey.

2. Journaling

Getting paid for something you love to do is a goal for most of us, but you need to figure out what that "something" is first!

That's a big reason why you should keep a journal. A well-kept journal becomes a daily discipline to help you keep track of your innermost thoughts and feelings. It is a very handy way to help you collect data to better formulate your interests, passions, and purpose and to stay intentional about pursuing and achieving your goals. It's essentially a personal accountability system, provided you take it seriously and allow for the time to review and rewrite the most significant parts. It will help you to review and deal with the hard facts during your essential periodic self-evaluations.

In December of 2016, I attended a professional development program, The Bartell and Bartell Leadership Flight School. The very first lesson on Day 1 of Flight School was taught by Dr. Bill Brashers and focused on the importance of Journaling. Bill said, "Experience is only valuable when lessons are learned." Journaling helps you to get the "ingredients" written down, which makes putting the formula together for a success plan much more probable down the road.

With all due respect to the folks who want you to believe achieving your dreams is as easy as just keeping a positive mindset, positivity is simply one part of making your dreams come true. A positive mindset is definitely needed, but it has to **form a partnership** with skill, hard work, a good plan, and persistence.

You must be deliberate in asking yourself: Is the dream attainable? Is it realistic? How long will it take? What path do you take to get there? Could it be attainable with the right plan and the right mentors in my life? You must also be committed to writing down your answers in your journal so the ideas don't simply vanish. This is the pragmatic, "keeping it real" part of Pragmatic Passion. It is "practical dreaming."

It's a part of your vision where you see yourself developing the necessary skills and knowledge to assist you in achieving your goals that will ultimately lead to living the life you desire.

"The happiest people are those who have found a way to get paid for something they would have done anyway!" **John Addison, Author, Real Leadership**

Objective 3: What Are Your Values and Interests?

"It's not hard to make decisions once you know what your values are." **Roy E. Disney, Senior Executive for The Walt Disney Company**

Values are what drive us internally in our decision-making process. It's a belief system that we use to determine what is right or wrong. It's how we determine what is important to us. This is your foundation, your core beliefs that will guide you in so many aspects of your life. Every day you take the "Mirror Test," where the person staring back at you is the one you must live with and be happy with daily. Socrates long ago said, "To know thyself is the beginning of wisdom." We know we are all flawed, and all make mistakes. Remember to forgive yourself, and others, and move on to reach your potential!

"Here are the values that I stand for: honesty, equality, kindness, compassion, treating people the way you want to be treated, and helping those in need. To me, those are traditional values." **Ellen DeGeneres, Actress and TV Host**

1. Pragmatic Passion Core Values

"Having a strong foundation based on values will keep you on the path to a joyful and fulfilling life. When you see tragedy, it usually comes back to abuse of power, excessive pleasure, or selfish pride that is a root cause. Let your core values guide your choices." **Dan Leri, Director of Innovation Park, Penn State**

Exploring, creating, and cultivating your passion and purpose is no easy task. You need to identify the most significant values to you. Ask yourself what matters most to you in life? These are your unique Pragmatic Passion Core Values and they are the foundation for living a joyful, successful life.

To assist in identifying your values, here's a short list of values to choose from (there's an in-depth list at **www.PragmaticPassion.com/bookresources**):

Authenticity	Drive
Autonomy	Empathy
Balance	Ethical
Common sense	Fame
Confidence	Fitness
Courage	Fun
Creativity	Gratitude
Curiosity	Growth
Dignity	Happiness
Discipline	Honesty

Kindness	Spirituality
Love	Status
Loyalty	Success
Meaningful	Transparency
Passion	Trust
Peace of Mind	Vision
Reputation	Wealth
Respect	Wisdom
Security	

This exercise is critical to building your foundation for your own Pragmatic Passion Vision Statement. Please take your time and give this some deep thought. Identifying your values will be the foundation upon which your purpose is built. No one can choose your values for you. This is a highly personal exercise for you to learn about values and to determine which are *currently* the most important to you.

To put you in the right frame of mind for this exercise, think about times in your life when you were the happiest. Think of when you did something that made you feel like you were an important part of a team or a positive contributor to an organization. Think of an event or accomplishment that made you feel great. Also think of times when you felt embarrassed or that you let a loved one down. If you can describe the feelings you felt, you are on your way to identifying the values that matter to you.

Using the list from above (or preferably the more detailed list online), write a list of **your personal top 10 values**:

1. _____   6. _____

2. _____   7. _____

3. _____   8. _____

4. _____   9. _____

5. _____   10. _____

When you have completed the review of the values list, rank the top five values that are most important to YOU and why. Go over this list with your Pragmatic Passion Partner and discuss them in depth to be sure that you are describing YOUR true feelings and not what you think others would want to hear from you.

1. _____

2. _____

3. _____

4. _____

5. _____

"We sacrifice our health in order to make wealth, then sacrifice our wealth in order to get back our health." **His Holiness the 14th Dalai Lama**

Consider what the Dalai Lama is saying and factor it into which values matter to you and why.

2. Interest, Personality, and Aptitude Assessments

"Knowledge is gained by gathering data, whereas, wisdom is earned by going through actual life experiences." **Master Jin Kwon, South Korean Martial Arts Master**

Identifying your interests is a critical part of self-discovery and will ultimately lead to a better alignment of what you like to do and your skills and knowledge. How does taking interest, personality, and aptitude assessments fit into determining your definition of success? It is another tool in your toolbox. Assessments, just like passion, are necessary, but not sufficient by themselves. These assessments can reveal and/or validate certain personality and behavioral traits that can help you align your interests and passions with a practical career track and life plan.

Pragmatic Point: Assessments are best utilized under the supervision of a professional career counselor who can properly interpret the results. Interests and passions can change with time, education, and action, so your stage of life is an important variable.

Cheryl Bonner is the Director of Alumni Career Services at Penn State and co-author of *Your Career Planner*. When I interviewed her she stated, "No assessment is going to point to the best career, job, or academic curriculum with 100% accuracy. Career counselors have differing opinions on the use of formalized assessments. Many see them as quick ways to help someone to achieve some self-understanding. Others see that users will interpret a result in isolation of other information in making a career decision." The assessments are tools. Not a "be all, end all" solution.

She went on to say, "However, the variety of formal and informal assessments allows for many types of self-discovery. Some will provide clues to preferred work environments, others to preferred skills to be used on the job, and others will suggest groupings of jobs based on interests."

Cheryl pointed out that utilizing counselors, self-directed books, and online tools could guide the user through a process of self-discovery and allow for the development of a realistic self-understanding that can then be used as a part of a career search. Counselors skilled in the use of assessments will help the user look for the reasons this career may have been suggested and then to use these insights in order to pick other careers more aligned with the total person.

Assessment results (properly evaluated for you by a professional) can provide several key insights for you such as:

1. Jump start you if you are really struggling to figure out what you are interested in and passionate about.

2. Help to validate what your own qualitative research is indicating and what you think you are interested in doing.

3. Assist in identifying your strengths and areas for improvement.

4. Guide you in selecting a post high school educational or training direction, a college major, and additional job training options for career advancement.

5. Reveal potential career paths.

Here are two free versions of assessments you can find online:

- For O*NET online go to: www.onetonline.org

- For My Next Move online go to: www.mynextmove.org

It is critical that when taking the assessments, that you be perfectly candid in answering the questions, so it most closely reflects your innermost feelings. Do not give answers that you believe others would want you to give. These are YOUR answers to aid you in getting started on a path toward finding a possible career path. As you grow as an individual, personality, interest, and aptitude assessments will be even more valuable in your twenties and beyond, after you have experienced the real world.

Real Life 101 – Why Using Professional Counselors Matters

When our youngest son, Ryan, was a junior in high school, we knew he was a terrific young man who possessed many strong qualities. He was, however, a perfectionist and despite doing extremely well in school and in sports, it never seemed to be good enough in his eyes. He would worry incessantly about whether he would be successful in school and life, constantly comparing himself to his older siblings. He would utter such self-deprecating comments as, "I will never be as successful as my brother and sister. I have no idea what I want to do with my life. Why go to college when I am probably going to fail." My initial instincts as a former coach were that this seemed a bit disingenuous and just a typical teenager being overly dramatic. But as a parent, this was our son, and we would take no chances in getting him assistance.

Ryan was taking almost all advanced courses as a junior at his high school, which is regarded as one of the best in the state of Pennsylvania. He carried a straight "A" average and won an academic award for his efforts in his Advanced U.S. history class as a sophomore, even though he tried his best to drop the class because it was so demanding. He also earned the number one spot on the boys' golf team. It seemed on the outside that everything was just fine; in fact it seemed great.

Despite all of this, he was more stressed out than I ever remember his siblings being in high school, and he was starting to show real signs of anxiety and depression. He lost his temper quickly, focused on the negative all the time, and spoke in terms of doom and gloom. In a September 2017 *Atlantic* magazine article, Professor Jean Twenge cited that the cases of teenage stress, anxiety, depression, and attempted suicides have reached record numbers (which she blames in large part on smartphone usage). Given this information, we felt it was time to intervene.

As parents, we did the best we could on our own, but inevitably we made the tough decision to have him seek professional help. First, we had him meet with Dr. Rod Bartell of Bartell and Bartell, organizational and leadership training experts. He was administered a personality assessment survey (one widely used among corporations), in addition to proprietary assessment tools. After going over the results with Dr. Bartell, Ryan was both relieved and much more confident about his future, as the results showed him a lot about himself, including several career paths that would align well with his interests and abilities.

Next, we sent him to meet with friend and clinical psychologist, Dr. Mike Wolff. After just two sessions with Mike to work on coping skills, and to just have someone other than mom and dad to talk to, we saw an amazing improvement in Ryan's demeanor and confidence in school and on the golf course. Four days later, he shot a 74, his lowest round ever in competition, and he won the Pennsylvania District 6 Sectional Championship.

Applying Dr. Stephen Covey's habit to "begin with the end in mind," I took Ryan out of school early one day to attend the Career Fair at the University. Under protest, he wore a suit and tie and carried a portfolio so he would blend in better. The purpose was to show him where all the hard work and focus studying would eventually lead him. I wanted him to see different careers and companies he had no idea existed and to broaden his horizons in the hopes he would realize that his worrying would dissipate with preparation. When I explained to an alumni volunteer why our high school junior was observing Career Fair, she told Ryan, "What a great idea!" and complimented him on his willingness to be assertive and forward thinking.

Ryan still has his moments when he gets too tough on himself, but overall, he is in a much better spot and we, as his parents, are much more comfortable and confident that he is in a good place.

The lessons learned from this experience?

1. Assessments can be a valuable tool to help give direction and build confidence, **when administered and followed up on by a professional**.

2. We all need coaches, mentors, friends, and family that are willing to assist in our times of need.

We recognized the need to get professionals involved to help our son through a tough spell. In Ryan's case, because of his age, we acted on his behalf utilizing our own skills and knowledge combined with our experience, which provided us the wisdom to intervene. **It was a win-win solution.** There are plenty of options for books, webinars, and counselors for professional career advice and coaching. This is such an important process for reaching your potential and living a fulfilling life, so give it the time and attention it deserves.

Find the courage and make the time to seek assistance if you determine it is needed. Put getting an assessment on your calendar right now!

3. What Are Your Natural Talents and Skills?

"A lot of people like to do certain things, but they're not that good at it. Keep going through the things that you like to do until you find something that you actually seem to be extremely good at. It can be anything." **George Lucas, Creator of Star Wars**

Have you ever mistaken interest for talent? Many people have. Your interests will be nothing more than idle wishes unless you first develop the skills and knowledge in order to have the ability to achieve your goals. This requires you to do what must be done to first acquire the skills and put yourself in a position to realistically achieve those goals.

We all have natural talents and skills that we have learned over the years. Some people are naturally artistic; some are great at math; some are great speakers; while others are great at building things.

What comes effortlessly to you? What did you love to do as a kid? List as many of the natural talents and skills you believe you possess.

Examples: Reading, running, starting a conversation, writing, solving puzzles, cooking, drawing, etc.

1. _____   6. _____

2. _____   7. _____

3. _____   8. _____

4. _____   9. _____

5. _____   10. _____

Now, ask your Pragmatic Passion Partner and three members of your Pragmatic Passion Advisors Team (see page 181) to list as many of the natural talents and skills THEY believe you have and compare the lists.

"We all have mirrors surrounding us that represent things we might be good at doing, and things we might not be good at doing. Hold up your mirrors and see where your own light shines and then have the confidence to unleash your talents."
Todd Erdley, CEO of Videon and Mentor of Entrepreneurs

4. What Are Your Concerns and Areas for Improvement?

Make a list of your most significant current concerns and fears.

Examples: Public embarrassment, getting a job, lack of confidence, meeting a soul mate, etc.

1. _____ _____

2. _____

3. _____

4. _____

5. _____

What do you consider to be areas of your life that need improvement? (These can be physical, mental, or spiritual.)

Examples: Understanding money, coping with stress, handling conflict, procrastination, etc.

1. _____

2. _____

3. _____

4. _____

5. _____

Objective 4: Develop Your Passions and Purpose

"Passion for your work is a little bit of discovery, followed by a lot of development, and then a lifetime of deepening." **Angela Duckworth, Best-Selling Author of Grit**

For many people, *purpose* is something they might search for their entire lives. Some may find their purpose yet, tragically, not recognize it, not act on it, or be dissuaded from naysayers to pursue it. And there are some who may go through several transformations with new and different passions and purposes. Let's try to determine yours at this particular stage of your life.

1. Explore your Passions and Causes

Too many people are alive but they don't really know how to *live*. Don't just be alive. Be passionate about life and learn how to truly live a vibrant existence. Passion **is your inner enthusiasm and energy toward life.** And it's critical to bring your passion to the key aspects of your life, your education, and your career.

I could not wait to get on the ice to play hockey, to coach hockey, to be with the players and staff, and to work together for the greater good of the team. My wife would remind me that she got up and went to work, while I leaped out of bed and went to play!

So, what does passion feel like to *you*? What do *you* care passionately about?

"Passion is a sense of exhilaration and excitement you will know only when you have experienced it. Don't expect to live a life of peak passion experiences everyday. We must learn to live the gaps between the peak experiences. The day to day disciplines that set you up for the percolations of moments of exhilaration." **Dennis Heitzmann, Ph.D., Child, Adult and Family Psychological Services**

Passion does not always reveal itself with an outward showing of energy, exuberance, and excitement. Passion is in your heart and soul and different people will display passion in different ways.

Passion Point: Passion is not the exclusive domain of extroverts.

In her best selling book, *Quiet: The Power of Introverts in a World That Can't Stop Talking*, author Susan Cain writes about the many strengths of those that society has labeled shy, quiet, and reserved. In her "Manifesto for Introverts," Susan points out that "Solitude is a catalyst for innovation," and that "One genuine relationship is worth a fistful of business cards."

Susan's book was a fascinating read for me since I am as extroverted as they come. Her take on the internationally famous self-help guru Tony Robbins, a bombastic, high-energy "Infotainer," really made me think of my own biases of how we recognize passion in someone. Just because someone isn't outwardly demonstrative doesn't mean they are not passionate about work, school, or life. Do not judge a book by its cover.

Exploring and discovering a passion that can be cultivated is part trial and error and part self-awareness.

Do you care about serving others less fortunate than you? Do you care about video games or technology? Do you care about nature and the outdoors? Do you care about music, animals, numbers, or drawing? Do you care about designing new buildings or watching college football? Are you passionate about making money? What do you care passionately about? Are you willing to embrace and cultivate that passion?

List at least five examples of what you are passionate about:

1. _____

2. _____

3. _____

4. _____

5. _____

Let's look at it another way. If money weren't an issue and if you knew you would be a raging success, what would you want to do with your life and why?

List at least five reasons that are holding you back from pursuing your dreams:

1. _____

2. _____

3. _____

4. _____

5. _____

List at least five examples of things you'd do if you knew you COULD NOT fail:

1. _____

2. _____

3. _____

4. _____

5. _____

"*Passion is the key to success. Passion is the difference-maker. You know why? Because people with passion, go above and beyond. They do what they have to do to get it right. They do what has to be done.*" **George Bodenheimer, Retired Disney Media Co-Chairman**

2. Your Desired Quality of Life: The Genie Test

There are no right or wrong answers here. You are simply trying to see where your thoughts take you when you think impulsively, and then, intentionally.

1. If you could seriously have any three wishes for your life, besides world peace, what would they be? Write the first three things that come to mind, quickly!

1. _____

2. _____

3. _____

2. If you could have just one wish, what would it be and why?

_____

_____

_____

Take a look at what you wrote. Did you take the exercise seriously? If not, why not?

3. Now go back and take your time. Think about your answers more deeply. If you could have any three wishes after some thought, what would they be and why?

1. _____

2. _____

3. _____

4. If you could have just one wish, what would it be and why?

_____

_____

_____

Did you perhaps write something to do with getting a great job, making a lot of money, having fame, or essentially extrinsic things? Some examples of answers you may not have considered are:

- A fulfilling life, full of joy, happiness, and great relationships

- A passion for learning

- Great health

- Financial independence to allow for philanthropic giving

- The flexibility to allow volunteering for my favorite cause

- A life full of adventure

"My wish? To have a loving family and friends." **Krishna Nadella, Americas Head of Sales for Portfolio Valuations, New Content, and Regulatory Solutions for Bloomberg L.P.**

When I first met Krishna he had just completed an MBA and was a Vice President at Citigroup based out of New York City. He was on the fast track in the global financial world. Life was good. Then the Great Recession of 2008 hit and he was one of thousands on Wall Street whose jobs were suddenly eliminated. Krishna never lost his faith and by leaning on his healthy relationships with family and friends, he not only persevered, he thrived. He is working for Bloomberg LP and is the creator, producer, and host of the web and TV-based discussion program, *STATE OF MIND with Krishna C. Nadella.*

What matters most to Krishna? "That I am honest with myself and my wife and engaged with my children and to have healthy societal relationships. If I have that, I can do anything."

The answers to all these exercises begin to provide you with information you need to make better choices for yourself in order to reach your goals. Consider changing your perspectives and focus more on a **higher purpose for your life**. I would bet in the long run you would be self-motivated to develop the necessary skills, the discipline, the determination, and the positive attitude to get that great job, make a substantial living, and perhaps gain a certain level of respect in your industry and community.

3. Determine your Purpose

"The purpose of life is not to be happy. It is to be useful, to be honorable, to be compassionate, to have it make some difference that you have lived and lived well." **Ralph Waldo Emerson**

So now that you have given deep thought to how you define success, what you are really interested in, what natural talents and skills you have, what values are meaningful to you and what you are truly passionate about, now it's time to begin to think more deeply about your **purpose**.

What legacy do you want to leave behind? What will they say about you when you are gone?

Your purpose should bring you and others happiness and joy and be bigger than anything you can accomplish by yourself.

Using your gifts for the greater good and to benefit others should be a major part of your own definition of success.

Passion Point: A Pragmatic Passion Challenge to you: Your purpose must be one of creating good in the world and helping others to do the same.

Remember, it is not enough to dream. **I'm going to insist that you drill deeper than that by continuing to ask yourself the hard questions that most people simply avoid. You must continuously explore and challenge yourself.** Put reminders right now on your calendar to do periodic self-evaluations. Determine the best cycle for you (monthly, quarterly, semi-annually) to intentionally review your plan.

This next exercise may open your eyes to options you never thought possible. Now, take what you have learned about yourself so far and give this your best effort. Remember that this is just a snapshot of where you are now. You can always come back and modify, improve, and stretch your aspirations!

At your induction into "The Greatest People in Society" ceremony, what would your biographical introduction say?

_____

_____

_____

_____

Who are the people that you would most like to pattern your life after and why?

1. _____

2. _____

3. _____

4. _____

5. _____

Passion Point: Passion must drive your purpose. There is a certain level of enthusiasm and energy that is necessary to change and improve.

When you combine your pragmatic self with your passionate self, you will find it much easier to discover your purpose.

Real Life 101 – When Passion Meets Purpose

Scott Shirley wanted to build buildings even as a young child. He was one of those rare kids who knew exactly what he wanted to do at a young age. In high school he was a standout student and football and baseball player. His father, Don, was a well-respected baseball coach and teacher who loved his family and was proud of his son. Scott realized two of his childhood dreams by playing college football at Penn State while earning his Civil Engineering degree.

After finishing his career as a Division I football player, Scott began his work as a civil engineer in Washington, D.C., living out his dream to build buildings. Unfortunately, his dad had a reoccurrence of kidney cancer, and after a valiant battle, Don passed away. Scott decided to commit himself to a career of helping those with rare diseases after tragically losing his father. He founded "Lift for Life," which started as a tribute to his father, and has blossomed into "Uplifting Athletes," a nonprofit organization that inspires the rare disease community with hope through the power of sports.

Scott has also become a successful entrepreneur based on his passion for helping others and his purpose for helping to treat rare diseases in honor of his father. In 2014 he founded PledgeIt.org, a start-up that raises awareness and funds for non-profits using "the power of sport for social good."

Scott has a passion and determination to serve others. He told me that one of his favorite quotes is from Aristotle. "Where your talents meet the needs of the world…therein lies your calling." He is a frequent public speaker and often challenges people to consider that their purpose is to make the world better by using their God-given talents to the best of their ability. "People can usually find their passion within if they consider serving the greater good."

Scott's goal of becoming an engineer was reached. But he found a new passion, a new cause, and a new purpose. Because of his strong family values, his father's inspiration, his passion for sports and helping others, and his purpose to help raise money and awareness for the rare disease community, Scott changed careers. He is a successful businessman, is married and raising a family. He is living a joyful, fulfilling life that would make his dad very proud.

Objective 5. Pragmatic Passion Personal Vision Statement

Now go back and review all your answers for the exercises in chapter one with your Pragmatic Passion Partner. Use what you have learned in this chapter about yourself and the life you envision, to formulate your own Pragmatic Passion Personal Vision Statement. Your statement can be as short or as long as you feel it takes to clearly describe your vision. To help you get started, here are a few examples below:

Real Life 101 – Personal Vision Statements:

Amanda Steinberg, founder of dailyworth.com:
"To use my gifts of intelligence, charisma, and serial optimism to cultivate the self-worth and net-worth of women around the world. I believe financially empowered women are the key to world peace."

Ryan Newman, Financial Services Executive:
"To be an ocean of inspiration and a well of giving set on the foundation of hard work, humility, and gratitude. To be a leader in my roles as: Father: 'Dad of wonder' / Husband: 'soulful listener' / Brother: 'advisor' / Son: 'net giver.'"

Joe Battista, Consultant, Success Coach, and Passioneer:
"To inspire and coach people to live joyful, fulfilling lives while serving others first and to form partnerships with other 'Passioneers' to make a positive impact for others. To care for my family and my own personal wellbeing, so I am healthy and energized to serve the greater good."

Ken "The Spice Man" Snyder, Ambassador for the Foundation for Free Enterprise Education:
"Be a positive influence to all whom I touch on the journey of life and bring unbridled passion via contagious enthusiasm in the inspiration of others to achieve their dreams. Through experience sharing and random acts of kindness, to live my life as a resource in service to all."

Krishna C. Nadella - Host & Producer of STATE OF MIND:
"To carry out my life in a fashion that my wife, children, family, and friends can be proud of and to leave an impact on this world that will allow others to craft the stories they want to present to the world. Every life is a book...make yours a bestseller!"

Erica Salowe, Recent College Graduate:
"Expand and capitalize on my natural writing and communications skills while pursuing a career in professional storytelling and brand building. To bring joy to others through my writing."

Real Life 101: Creating A Pragmatic Passion Vision Statement

Recent College Graduate Erica
Salowe's Adventure Awaits!
[*Courtesy of Sarah Snyder
Photography*]

I interviewed Erica Salowe, a recent college graduate, who earned a degree in Public Relations and English, with a minor in International Studies, to help her create her vision statement. We went over her answers to the exercises in Chapter 1 and together, authored her Pragmatic Passion Vision Statement.

Values: Honesty, loyalty, effort, ambition

Interests: Writing, reading (fiction/fantasy; favorite is Graceling series), action movies, fun with friends, college prep (stressful time, practiced SAT and filled out many college apps), listening to Celtic music, travel

NOT Interested In: Math/science/technology

Skills & Knowledge: AP English/History/Spanish, honors classes in the humanities

Natural Talents/What You Do Well: Writing, people person, being "the mom" (common sense), surrounding herself with good people, vivid imagination, ambitious, external supportive family/network, spiritual/not religious

What Others Say You Do Well: Good writer, driven, fortunate

Concerns/Areas for Improvement: Hypercritical, perfectionist, worrier, procrastinator, cares about what others say, hard worker and hard on herself, lacks confidence

Passions: Family, travel, hiking, adventurer, Scotland + Celtic culture. Dream is to be a best-selling author. Majors in Public Relations to pay the bills--career in professional storytelling

Causes: Four Diamonds Dance Marathon (THON) benefiting Pediatric Cancer Patients

Quality of Life Desired: Create enjoyable moments--traveling, memories with family, lots of laughs and intellectual conversation. To comfortably afford a sizable, nicely decorated home, perhaps a vacation home. To afford things I need and many things that I want. I believe however, that true happiness can't be measured by material possessions alone.

Stage of Life: Recent college graduate

Personal Vision Statement: "Expand and capitalize on my natural writing and communications skills while pursuing a career in professional storytelling and brand building. To bring joy to others through my writing."

Using the examples in this chapter and the help of your Pragmatic Passion Partners, formulate your own Pragmatic Passion Personal Vision Statement:

_____

_____

_____

_____

_____

Chapter 1 Summary:

1. To go from self-discovery to self-realization

2. To define what success looks like for you

3. To help you determine your values and interests

4. To help you develop your passion and purpose

5. To write your Pragmatic Passion Personal Vision Statement

Now that we covered these five objectives, it's time to do a "snapshot" of where you are today in your quest and answer these questions:

1. What does success look like for YOU?

_____

_____

_____

2. What are your Top 5 values?

_____

_____

_____

3. What are you most interested in?

_____

_____

_____

4. What are you most passionate about?

_____

_____

_____

5. What have you learned about your life purpose?

_____

_____

_____

"Your purpose explains what you are doing with your life. Your vision explains how you are living your purpose. Your goals enable you to realize your vision." **Bob Proctor, Best Selling Author, Proctor-Gallagher Institute**

Chapter 2
Attitude

"I am convinced that life is 10% what happens to me and 90% how I react to it. And so it is with you...we are in charge of our attitudes."

Charles Swindoll, Author and Educator

Chapter 2 Objectives:

1. To Have an Awesome Attitude

2. To Practice Common Courtesy & Mutual Respect

3. To learn to T.A.G. people daily using "The Attitude of Gratitude"

4. To take **C.H.A.R.G.E** of YOUR life

We spent Chapter 1 defining success for you, visualizing a life you desire, identifying your interests and passions, and learning about what's important to you as you search for your purpose. In this chapter we will focus on the attitudes you need to fulfill your destiny.

I see **attitude** as your mental outlook and approach to everything you do. It's your level of self-confidence, a level of emotional maturity, and a level of effort toward something or someone.

Objective 1: Have an Awesome Attitude

So, how important is the right attitude in achieving success? Well, a recent Stanford Research Institute study stated the path to success is comprised of 88% attitude and only 12% education. Seems Charles Swindoll has Stanford researchers supporting his beliefs.

Now don't misinterpret their findings. We all know how important education is and the point of the research is that knowledge alone is not nearly as effective without the right attitude to power you through your journey.

We all face challenges in life every day. **How you respond makes all the difference.**

When you woke up this morning, did you hit the snooze button several times and finally say…*"Oh well, guess I better get up and drag myself to work (or school)."*

Or did you jump out of bed when the alarm rang, look in the mirror and say…*"It's me and you against the world, when do we attack!"*

Admittedly, a positive attitude is not all you need. It is essential, but not the only character trait needed. You still need passion. You need skills and knowledge. But having a positive attitude is an important piece of the puzzle that I believe is critical to your success.

I have come across far too many people who still believe that talent and talent alone is paramount to achieving success in business, careers, sports, and life. Every cell in my body tells me this could not be further from the truth.

Passion Point: As a Passioneer I believe that a positive attitude, passion, persistence, and perseverance are the true difference makers to achieving personal and professional success.

Yes, talent matters, especially if you want to be a brain surgeon, rocket scientist, pro athlete, or play in a world-class orchestra. But even in those occupations you will never reach the peak of your craft without a great work ethic and positive attitude. For the rest of us, having a great attitude can assist with the deficiencies we may have with our current skill set and help us tremendously along our journey.

I have heard the following phrase from coaches, teachers, and professional athletes over and over again: *"Hard work beats talent when talent doesn't work hard!"*

There's no doubt about it...attitude is a choice. **You** have the ability to choose your attitude toward everything in your life, so why not choose to make it **awesome.**

"To change your life, you have to change the way you think. Behind everything you do is a thought. Every behavior is mo-

tivated by a belief. Every action is promoted by an attitude. Your life is directed by your thoughts!" **John Wright, CEO of Greyfield Legacies**

Objective 2: Common Courtesy and Mutual Respect

In a 2017 article in the Business Insider, writer Kate Taylor reported that Chick-fil-A is beating every competitor by simply training workers to say "please" and "thank you." This seems like such a basic concept, but this courteous interaction is facing extinction with everyone's heads buried in their cellphones. **This simple gesture is an easy opportunity for you to differentiate yourself from the crowd.**

Practicing common courtesy and mutual respect IS a simple concept but it is not emphasized nearly enough in today's schools, homes, and workplaces. Here are two rules to consider adopting into your personal approach to life:

> **The Golden Rule:** *"Treat others as you would want to be treated."*

> **The Platinum Rule:** *"Treat others as THEY would want to be treated."*

The platinum rule takes into account cultural differences and recognizes context and empathy as an important aspect of how to treat others regardless of gender, age, ethnicity, spirituality, and race. Treat people well, like they are the guest of honor or a VIP. Put your own ego aside.

My experiences tell me that attitude starts with self-respect. If you don't respect yourself and hold yourself to high standards, how can you expect anyone else to respect you? If you walk around with a miserable and cynical demeanor all day, who would want to spend time with you? If you have an attitude of entitlement and simply expect things to be handed to you without really earning it, what message does that send to your family, friends, and employer?

Passion Point: Be the *victor*, not the *victim*!

Most of us have times when we slip into "pity-party" mode and feel the need to "play the blame game" and blame every failure on someone else or on circumstances beyond our control. Do not allow yourself to linger for much time in the victim role. A strong mind and positive attitude will minimize the time spent there. Instead, always strive to be the victor and start working on confronting your challenges and on ways to overcome your circumstances with a better attitude.

"Never tell your problems to anyone...20% don't care and the other 80% are glad YOU have them." **Lou Holtz, Hall of Fame NCAA Football Coach and Analyst**

We are all dependent on relationships with others to achieve both personal and professional success. So the attitudes we bring into every relationship are critical - especially when dealing with difficult people or those we may simply not care to be around. I can trace most of my failures and disappointments back to having a bad attitude in dealing with people in my life. Almost every time, in retrospect, I was in the wrong. I still work on this daily and while I lapse, I find better outcomes when I am intentional in controlling my emotions and demeanor.

One of my best friends and mentors, Lt. Colonel Dick Bartolomea, taught us the correct way to treat others: "When dealing with people…be fair, firm, consistent, and treat them with **dignity**!"

I heard an impactful presentation at an American Hockey Coaches Association Conference by performance consultant Dr. Cynthia Adams Harrison about group dynamics. She gave out a hockey puck that to this day is displayed in my office. The side facing outward toward the person meeting with me says, "Egos Don't Win Championships, Teammates Do!" The side that I look at every day says, "Great Coaches know when to lead, and when to get out of the way!" There is no room for self-serving egos on your team.

Common courtesy and mutual respect means that if we are going to be great, we need to be great together. Jim Collins, author of the best selling business book, *Good to Great*, says that EGO stands for "Eases Greatness Out." It is a reminder that we all need to be "other-centered" and not self-centered.

Objective 3: The Attitude of Gratitude

Smiling and saying thank you are both easy and free and they pay big dividends. These simple acts of authentic kindness can make someone's day and require so little effort. It is so difficult to accomplish anything of value by yourself. You need a team of advisors who help you through key stages of your life. How often do you go back and say "thank you" to a former teacher, coach, relative, or classmate that may have helped you in either small or transformative ways? Well, now you are going to make it a priority.

It is essential for you to understand the importance of having "**The Attitude of Gratitude**" and to remember to frequently "**T.A.G.**" the people who have made a positive difference in your life. I would suggest setting up a time once a week in your calendar to remind you to T.A.G. the positive difference -makers in your life.

I have "The Attitude of Gratitude" so today I am going to thank _____.

Pick out someone in each of the following categories who have made a positive difference in your life or career. T.A.G. them with a personalized thank you message. Who will you T.A.G. today?

- Personal life (family and friends)

- Mentors (teachers, professors, advisors)

- Professional life (supervisors, colleagues, clients)

How do you T.A.G. someone?

1. Text...quick and easy (therefore, NO excuses!)

2. Email...fast and allows for a little more formal greeting.

3. Call...it's much more personal.

4. Write a letter...deeper thought, lasting impression, and a pleasant surprise!

5. Visit them in person...**the very best option!** Look the person in the eye and tell them what they have meant to you.

To be intentional in remembering to reach out periodically to say thank you, put a T.A.G. reminder in your calendar right now.

Objective 4: Take C.H.A.R.G.E. of YOUR Life!

"Whether you think you can, or you think you can't - you're right." **Henry Ford, Automaker**

You really are what you think you are! I believe you can choose your attitude, so it's better to choose a positive one! I realize we can't always be positive. Trust me, I have gone negative and lacked self-confidence enough times in both my personal and professional lives and have almost always lived to regret it. It is hard enough to deal with the negativity from others, it makes no sense to go inwardly negative and sabotage your own attitudes, and perhaps sabotage your own success.

Pragmatic Point: Ambition counts for nothing until it forms a partnership with hard work, a positive attitude, and action!

One strategy for keeping a positive attitude is to take **C.H.A.R.G.E** of your life! By implementing these 5 attributes you will find it easier to avoid self-doubt and stay focused on controlling your "controllables."

Commitment

Honor

Action

Respect

Grit

Enthusiasm!

Commitment: You must make a commitment to work toward your purpose and passion. After you have read this book and completed the exercises, I encourage you to make a commitment to achieving success in your life. To help you formalize your commitment, I've created a simple contract for you. You can find it at **www.PragmaticPassion.com/ bookresources** Sign the contract, take a picture of the contract, and send a copy of your contract to your Pragmatic Passion Partner so they can help you with your new mission.

"Many people don't focus enough on execution. If you make a commitment to get something done, you need to follow through on that commitment." **Kenneth Chenault, CEO of American Express Corporation**

Honor: Resolve to be a person of honor and integrity. How? By making every decision with the "Google Alert" or "Front Page" test in mind. For example, if you knew in advance that your choices were illegal, unethical, harmful to others, or simply the wrong thing to do, and a story about your actions would appear on the internet, in social media, or in the print media, would you still make that choice? If you can answer

"NO" to these questions, then you pass the tests with honor and integrity.

"Real Integrity is doing the right thing, knowing that nobody's going to know whether you did it or not." **Oprah Winfrey, actress, producer, businesswoman**

Action: "Get Into The Action Habit!" You **have** to take action. A lot of people have dreams and ambitions, and then talk a big game about what they are going to do. Ambition counts for nothing until it forms a partnership with a positive attitude, hard work, and action! Stop procrastinating! "Perfect" is often the enemy of "done!"

"A good plan executed well in a timely manner is better than the perfect plan acted upon too late." **World War II U.S. General George S. Patton**

Respect: Have the self-respect that allows you to be a person who respects all things and all people. You have to learn to respect yourself, believe in yourself, and surround yourself with people who respect you and will encourage you and help make you a better person.

"We don't need to share the same opinions as others, but we need to be respectful." **Taylor Swift, Grammy Winning Singer/Songwriter**

Grit: Have the intentional daily discipline of mental toughness and persistence to create the habits that keep your journey moving forward. Be a "grinder," as we say in hockey, and work determinedly through the temporary setbacks you will inevitably face. In other words, do the hard things, the things you may not want to do, knowing you are a better person for doing them.

"What we accomplish in the marathon of life depends tremendously on our grit, our passion and perseverance for long-term goals. An obsession with talent distracts us from that simple truth." **Angela Duckworth, Author of Grit**

Enthusiasm: Have the enthusiasm to inspire others and make things happen. Believe me, speaking as a parent, a coach, and a leader, it is hard to influence others and get anything worthwhile accomplished without enthusiasm. We are naturally drawn to people who exhibit enthusiasm in their daily lives, whether it's for work or for play.

"Enthusiasm is one of the most powerful engines of success. When you do a thing, do it with all your might. Put your whole soul into it. Stamp it with your own personality. Be active, be energetic, be enthusiastic and faithful, and you will accomplish your objective. Nothing great was ever achieved without enthusiasm." **Ralph Waldo Emerson, Philosopher and Poet**

Real Life 101: The Infectious Power Of A Positive Attitude

A former colleague of mine with the Buffalo Sabres, security officer James McDuffie, is one of the happiest and most gregarious employees who worked at the Sabres Arena. Every day he said hello with energy, enthusiasm, and an infectious smile and made everyone who came into the security area feel genuinely welcome. You would have never suspected the violent and dreadful past James was able to escape from to become a beloved employee and colleague because of his positive attitude, grit, and perseverance.

James overcame various personal and family setbacks in his life but succeeded in getting out of the "Little Vietnam" section of the east side of Buffalo, where gangs, drugs, death, and despair reigned. Like many inner-city kids, he found a temporary respite in sports as a football player. But after being told he could not play because of a heart condition, he began to act out and was kicked out of school. His father told him, "I'm not going to let a bum live in my house. Go get a job!"

Buffalo Sabres security officer James McDuffie,
"The Vice President of Hugs," known for his
infectious smile and positive attitude.

James enrolled in a work program and earned his GED. He did find various jobs, but he also got in with the wrong crowd of friends. Excessive drinking and fighting ensued and ultimately cost him his first marriage to a woman he now realizes was just trying to help him become a better person. Six of his childhood friends died from unhealthy lifestyles consumed by drugs, alcoholism, smoking, and violence.

James knew he had to change his attitude in order to change his life. He told me that on November 13, 1993 he reached his tipping point. "I knew it was time to take charge of my life and make a commitment to become a better man." He gave up drinking and smoking (he hasn't done either since!) and he got a job as a security guard at a bank. He started working security for the Sabres in 1996 and has been there ever since.

He credits his change in attitude and his faith for transforming his life. "My mom planted the seed for my faith as a kid." With a big smile he said, "It just took a while to sprout!" He added, "I honor my mom's memory with my passion for studying the Bible."

"I've met a President, senators, singers, comedians, and star athletes. I even played Ping-Pong with Phil Collins. I saw the Stanley Cup be awarded. That was all great, but it is my personal relationships with the people in my life and with God that have given me strength and endurance."

"I am who I am. I don't try to impress people. I try to treat everyone with respect. I just try to be myself." His enthusiasm is so infectious. He is the self-professed "Vice President of Hugs" and his philosophy is to "get to know everyone who comes into the building and treat each one well."

By applying a daily positive attitude, practicing "The Attitude of Gratitude," by taking **C.H.A.R.G.E.** of his life, and by having a strong passion for his faith, James found a way out of a hellacious environment and violent past. He not only persevered, he has found his passion and his purpose in serving others. "Despite all my defects and imperfections, I have found happiness. I am happy and at peace." That sounds like personal and professional success to me.

Chapter 2 Summary:

1. To Have an Awesome Attitude

2. To Practice Common Courtesy & Mutual Respect

3. To learn to T.A.G. people daily using "The Attitude of Gratitude"

4. To take **C.H.A.R.G.E** of YOUR life

Now that you have learned about the importance of courtesy, respect, gratitude, and your attitude, answer these questions:

1. Give an example of when you used common courtesy and mutual respect in a positive way?

_____

_____

_____

2. What people did you T.A.G. today, what delivery method did you choose, and what was their reaction?

_____

_____

_____

3. How have you taken charge of your life lately and what positive, new daily habits are you adding?

_____

_____

_____

4. Give an example of when you were persistent and your persistence paid off. Give an example where you were stubborn beyond a practical level and you reached a point of futility before "pivoting" for a better result?

_____

_____

_____

5. Give an example of when you (or someone close to you) persevered over time and achieved a significant goal.

_____

_____

_____

"Your beliefs become your thoughts. Your thoughts become your words. Your words become your actions. Your actions become your habits. Your habits become your values. Your values become your destiny." **Mahatma Gandhi**

Chapter 3
Sacrifice

"Human progress is neither automatic nor inevitable...
Every step toward the goal of justice requires sacrifice,
suffering, and struggle; the tireless exertions and
passionate concern of dedicated individuals."

Martin Luther King, Jr.

Chapter 3 Objectives:

1. To use "The Power of Focus"

2. To manage your time. Say a polite "No" so you can get to your "Yes"

3. Passion, Persistence, and Perseverance Matter

We discussed in the last chapter whether you were going to have the attitude of a victim or a victor. Life is hard at times. It is not always fair. But if you are willing to stay faithful to your values, build a solid foundation of skills and knowledge, and make the right sacrifices at the right times in your life, you can persevere through even the toughest challenges and adversities.

You were introduced to the Pragmatic Passion logo earlier in the book. I said those who see the "D" get bonus points. That "D" stands for **disciplined determination**. The kind of self-discipline required to resist impulsive feelings and emotions is a key part of the will to make the necessary sacrifices to succeed.

Objective 1: The Power of Focus

"A Jedi must have the deepest commitment, the most serious mind." **Yoda, Jedi Master in Star Wars - The Empire Strikes Back**

The above quote is from one of the most impactful scenes in what many critics dub the best *Star Wars* movie in franchise history, *The Empire Strikes Back*. Jedi Master Yoda attempts to teach his young apprentice, Luke Skywalker, the importance of being disciplined and staying focused on the task at hand. He reminds him to pay deliberate attention to the present.

Yoda continued, "All his life has he looked away...to the future, to the horizon. Never his mind on where he was."

Mindfulness is *intentional* attention on the present. Intentional meaning purposeful, deliberate, conscious, and planned. This has never been more important than in today's mega-distracted world. You need to stay focused on the task at hand and live more in the moment. Given my personality profile as a social person with high energy and vision, I struggle mightily with this myself and find that I have always been at my best when I find a way to be deliberate in my focus. I also needed the help of my wife, my mentors, and especially any staff assistant who ever had to help me stay focused! My wife loves to say, "Any fool can handle a crisis, it's the day-to-day stuff that's hard!"

Long ago Confucius stated, "Remember, no matter where *you* go, there you are." My first time hearing this was at a coaches' clinic in Lake Placid, NY from sports psychologist Dr. Paul Klein. He reminded us that we are the same people with the same set of skills whether we play at home or on the road, in a regular season contest or a championship game. His message was one of self-confidence in the moment. Believe in yourself, stay focused, and control what's controllable. You take your DNA with you whether you are going to school, on a business trip, or on a job interview.

"In an on-demand, 24/7 society, where distractions cost millions of people productivity, profitability, relationships and peace, it's time to pay attention to what matters most." **Neen James, Author of Attention Pays**

It is probably no surprise to you that as a Passioneer, I love movies and books that tell inspiring stories of adventure and overcoming odds. The original *Star Wars* movie, which came out during my junior year of high school, was a big inspiration. The now-famous scene of a young Luke Skywalker staring off into the future resonated with me at that exact time in my life. *Star Wars: A New Hope* was far different than any movie previously produced, and it challenged the status quo that science fiction was outside the mainstream. Its popularity has endured over several generations of fans, and new feature films and books are still being created.

This is a testament not only to the vision of Director George Lucas, but equally as important are the sacrifices and the powerful focus made by Lucas and the thousands of people who have helped him make the movies a reality. It was in large part George's laser focus (pun intended!) that made the Star Wars franchise the most successful in motion picture history.

There is a little Luke Skywalker in all of us, especially when we are young and so uncertain, or when we are going through a transition phase of our lives. Staying focused requires the self-discipline to be intentional on a daily basis and to surround yourself with people who will assist in helping you remain on task.

Think of a time when you were laser focused on a goal and it led to a successful conclusion.

Write down your answer here:

_____

_____

_____

Now, think of a time when you allowed yourself to be distracted and it led to disappointment or, even worse, where you allowed "excusitis" to set in and you placed the blame on someone else.

Write down your answer here:

_____

_____

_____

Finally, take a minute to think of the corrective actions you might have taken to avoid that disappointment.

Write down your answer here:

_____

_____

_____

1. "Keep your eye on the prize!"

"I still have my eyes on the prize: I want to be that old lady onstage shaking her hips and singing her greatest hits." **Christina Aguilera, Grammy Award winning Singer and Producer**

Do you ever find yourself bouncing between different goals, dreams, and passions and never feel like you are truly committed and focused on making any real progress? After all, just because you are doing *something* does not mean you are moving forward.

Academy Award winner Denzel Washington says, "Do not confuse activity with productivity. You can run in place as hard as you want and not get anywhere." You can't "major in minors," getting caught up doing a bunch of meaningless tasks that take your focus away from your priorities, and expect to achieve your biggest, most transformational goals.

To make a dream come true, you must be fully committed to it and concentrate on it, and to focus your energy and effort into doing something about it daily. Yes, you need to take care of the routine tasks that come with everyday living, but don't let the small stuff derail you from your primary target. Be as efficient as possible with your daily list of tasks so you can get to the juicy, growth-oriented items on your list. Setting priorities and paying attention to the most significant goals on your list is how to become successful in achieving your dreams.

A few members of my own Pragmatic Passion Advisory Team include retired executive Pete Rohrer and retired media expert Rod Burnham. They are volunteers from S.C.O.R.E., an organization of retired executives that assist start-ups and entrepreneurs. During one of our breakfast meetings, Pete looked me right in the eye and said, "You have too much on your plate. You have to make some tough choices and get focused. *Just finish something!*"

I have to tell you, those words stung, but I needed to hear them. I immediately set forth a plan to follow his sage advice. It included having to say no to a number of people and opportunities in an effort to get more focused on my prize. It is this type of brutally honest feedback and advice that makes all the difference, provided that the receiver avoids getting defensive. When receiving the feedback that is intended to assist, you must have the self-confidence to "hear what you must hear," so you can "do what you must do" to improve and grow as a person and a professional.

In her book, *Attention Pays*, Author Neen James talks about the importance of staying focused and paying attention. The benefits of "unplugging" from the daily barrage of disruptions of social media and "plugging" into the tools, strategies, and a focused mindset that allow you to get your work done on the road to achieving success.

"If you don't give 100% of yourself, someone, somewhere, will and they will be better prepared and they will beat you." **Former U.S. Senator Bill Bradley, NBA Hall of Famer**

Real Life 101 – "When you cross the line, nothing else matters!"

In my 10th season as Head Coach at Penn State, we hired a young, bold assistant coach named Scott Balboni, who helped re-energize our program, and me as a coach. One of the great inspirational sayings he brought with him from Providence College was, "When you cross the line, nothing else matters!"

It was a quote about focus and paying attention to the task at hand. If you "cross the line" by walking into a classroom or the library, then study, don't socialize, check email, surf the web, or think about practice or the big game coming up. This is time to focus on academics and clear your mind of any other issues, most of which you have no control over. It is the same with family time and time with friends. Give them your focused attention.

We actually painted a white line on the flooring just before the players entered the ice surface for practice and games. It was their cue that for the next 90 minutes it was time to focus on hockey and not worry about their next test or homework assignment or think about their social plans. That team won a National Championship *and* set a new team record for academic success in the classroom. Many of those players still talk about the impact that the "crossing the line" message makes in their lives. Alumnus Jason Zivkovic, an attorney in Pittsburgh, told me that he still thinks of that saying every time he steps into a courtroom. "In my professional life, just like in hockey, it takes a focused mind to be at my best. Crossing that line before entering the courtroom is that reminder that it's game on."

So when you "cross the line" by walking into a conference room for a seminar, then listen intently, don't check Twitter or think about some big project back at the office. If you "cross the line" to go into someone's office for a meeting, then give them your undivided attention. If you "cross the line" to go to a class, then stay focused on the material you are learning.

You must focus, and you must learn to sacrifice some things so you can be focused. You must improve your mental toughness to stay on target. Remember Michael Hyatt's quote from Chapter 1, "You can do anything you want...you just can't do everything you want!"

1998 ACHA National Championship Team

2. School/Work/Life Integration

Because it takes an intense desire and a laser focus to achieve most worthwhile goals, I have come to realize that "School/Work/Life Balance" is a very elusive reality, especially for anyone wanting to realistically make positive changes and go after a transformative dream. A better description for the elusive work-life balance is work-life integration. To achieve even a single significant goal or a milestone in pursuit of your dream requires tremendous sacrifices to be made.

Do not fool yourself. The commitment to deliberate, disciplined, hard work is non-negotiable. You WILL sacrifice leisure time or idle hours by spending focused time on your goals. You must be willing to give up some distractions to stay laser focused. The reward will be worth it! If you are truly pursuing one of your passions, and they align with your purpose, you may not even feel like you are working.

In my interview with Jeffrey Hayzlett, CEO of the C-Suite Network and best selling author, he cut right to the chase. "It's called hard work for a reason. It's hard. It takes time and sacrifices. It's what pays the bills. When my kids would say they wished I could be home more often, I would simply say, okay, what do you want to cut out that you like to do? They understood that it was my dedication that allowed us to have our quality of life. You just realistically can't have it all. We all have a finite amount of time, energy, and ability and must choose what we want from it." I think what Jeffrey is saying is that it's really a "life-work integration" and not *balance* that should be the pragmatic goal.

When you seem to lose track of time because you are so focused, you have achieved what many psychologists refer to as a "state of flow." You will know when you are "in the flow" because it will become subconscious. You won't want to stop because you are "in the zone" and "on a roll."

I found myself leaving the hockey office at 1 or 2 o'clock in the morning feeling bummed out because I had to end the workday. Yes, it was still a job, but it was purposeful and I was passionate and believed that the extra sacrifice made all the difference.

Plenty of articles have been written about "having it all." I am not advocating an unhealthy work plan, as you will certainly need your rest, relaxation, and exercise to go along with your mental work.

Remember *Arête*, the perfect blending of body, mind, and spirit. You must learn how much you can push your body, mind, and spirit to create the positive change you want in your life. Keep in mind, this must take into account your stage of life and your current financial status as well.

Objective 2: Saying "No" to Get to Your "Yes"

"The important thing is this: to be able, at any moment, to sacrifice what we are for what we could become." **Maharishi Mahesh Yogi**

You have no doubt heard someone say that life is not a sprint, but a marathon. It requires patience, hard work, focused determination, and the ability to manage your time.

What does it mean to make a sacrifice? It most often means saying "no" to something you really like in order to get to the "yes" of completing another, more important goal along the way to your dreams.

I can guarantee that you WILL have to say "no" to a lot of people, to fun activities, to perhaps some live music or sporting events, and most definitely to excess wasted time on social media, in order to say "yes" to the steps it takes to achieve success.

Real Life 101 – A Purpose That Required The Sacrifice Of A Passion

Vincent "V.J." Nardy was very passionate about hockey, the sport that taught him the value of hard work, sacrifice, discipline, and teamwork. He loved the camaraderie of being with his Penn State teammates and the physical discipline of playing a team sport that he had enjoyed since he was five years old.

Like so many college students, V.J. was unsure of his major as a freshman and it was a meeting with his hockey team academic advisor Ruth Hussey, a professional guidance counselor, that helped him realize his interest, skills, and passion for the life sciences. He discovered his purpose was to serve others as a medical doctor. But as his class load and the time required to study increased, V.J. also reached a pivotal point in his life when he realized his passion for his sport was possibly interfering with his ultimate dream of being a surgeon.

V.J. went through a very tough time emotionally when he realized he needed to spend more time studying in order to earn the grades needed to get into medical school. Something had to give. After a heart-wrenching talk with his father, he realized for the first time the final result would be that competitive hockey might have to come to an end. V.J. sat down with me to discuss his situation. It was a very emotional talk in my office, and when we were done, he made the incredibly hard, courageous, and mature decision to take the remainder of the season off, leaving open the possibility of a return if he changed his mind.

"I had been a hockey player my whole life. At the time, it defined me. But deep down, I knew this was what I had to do. I had to make this sacrifice to achieve my goal of being a doctor."

He also realized he needed assistance and had the foresight and fortitude to ask for help. We set him up with a tutor for his very difficult Organic Chemistry classes, who was also his tutor for his Medical College Aptitude Test. In 2007, V.J. Nardy began medical school. In 2011 he became Dr. Vincent J. Nardy! He completed his time as a fellow in Cardiothoracic Surgery at Ohio State University in July of 2018 and became an attending Cardiothoracic Surgeon in Dayton, Ohio.

1. Delayed Gratification

"If it wasn't hard, everyone would do it. It's the hard that makes it great." **Tom Hanks to Geena Davis in A League of Their Own**

How good are you at just saying "no" to impulsive temptations? In our consumer dominated world, there is a growing desire for all things bigger, better, and faster. Instant gratification and a false sense of entitlement threaten the achievement of the real success we desire. We have become a society of "I want this, and I want it right now!" You must learn the virtues of self-control, patience, and willpower. Short-term gains are often at the expense of far more long lasting and more valuable rewards, unless we make sacrifices in the "now." Embrace the strategy and the rewards of delayed gratification.

In basic economics, we are taught the concept of *opportunity cost.*

For every decision you make, there is a sacrifice being made for something else you might have done with that time, money, and energy. This is *opportunity cost.* If you choose to spend all your time on social media with friends or binge watching the latest Netflix series, it comes at a cost. If you take the time to go to the movies or play golf with your friends too often, it will cost you time and money. Instead of wasting time and money on impulsive acquisitions, what if you spent the time and money on more meaningful activities and resources that will help you achieve your goals?

Since you've decided to go on a Pragmatic Passion Journey, you made a commitment to get out of the "sea of sameness," ignore the conventional wisdom, and be unique. That means having the courage to do what must be done, when it needs to be done. This includes shutting off your electronics, delaying the purchase of a want, and learning to say a polite "no" to people who are disrupting your focus and leading you away from your goals.

There is real gratification and satisfaction that can come from a hard days work, and "just" doing your job, that we often dismiss or discount. Bring your passion with you every day and take pride in your work, regardless of what you do. Derive happiness from giving it your best effort on a consistent basis. It could lead to opportunities as you gain a reputation as a person who gets things done.

Pragmatic Point: What are you willing to do more of, do differently, and stop doing now to drive improvement through your life to achieve your personal and professional dreams?

When you can answer that question, then you will know what it really means to make sacrifices. Using a "delayed gratification" mindset, take a moment now and list some of the sacrifices you know you need to make, and the habits you need to change to improve:

1. _____

2. _____

3. _____

4. _____

5. _____

"The single most important distinction in life...is to distinguish between an opportunity to be seized and a temptation to be resisted." **Rabbi Lord Jonathan Sacks**

2. Time Management Strategies

"The key is not to prioritize what's on your schedule, but to schedule your priorities." **Dr. Stephen Covey**

There are 24 hours in a day, 168 hours in a week, and 8,736 hours in a year. If you live to the median current life expectancy of 82 (in the U.S.), you will have 718,320 hours for this journey we call life. However, if you sleep for one-third of your life (8 hours/night) and you spend 80,000 hours at work (40 hours/week for 50 weeks – 2 weeks of vacation – for 40 years), then you're down to just under 400,000 hours. Let that sink in for a moment, *but just a moment*, as we have to keep moving and be efficient with our time!

So, if we only have a finite amount of time, then we must be deliberate and intentional with our time as it is one of the most valuable commodities over which we have significant control! You must commit to learning time management and developing the discipline to follow through if you are to achieve your goals and fulfill your purpose with passion.

In a recent survey by Salary.com, 89% of respondents admitted to wasting time every day at work including 31 percent who said they waste roughly 30 minutes daily and another 31 percent who waste one hour daily. There were as many as 6 percent who said they waste up to three hours daily!

How are people wasting time? A 2017 Thought.com article titled "The Top 10 Ways of Wasting Time in College" could easily represent timewasters for most age groups.

1. Social Media (Instagram, Snapchat, Twitter, Facebook)

2. People (just hanging out, gossiping)

3. The World Wide Web (pointless surfing)

4. The Party Scene (unhealthy behaviors)

5. Drama (unnecessary involvement with others' issues)

6. Email (checking too often, answering unimportant messages)

7. Cell Phone (texting too often, taking photos of everything)

8. Movies/You Tube (watching whatever is on or useless shows)

9. Video Games (playing for too long and too late into the night)

10. Lack of Sleep (loss of focus, emotional health issues)

Tom Westfall, one of my former players, said that the most important non-hockey skill he learned in college was **managing his time**. We offered every player a time management template to help them be organized and to plan out their days, weeks, and months. Some took advantage of this, while others did not. Some were naturally better at time management and prioritizing, while others needed guidance and tools to help them.

Personally, time management is still a challenge for me because I care about people and too often believe I can positively impact everyone who asks for my help. While it sounds noble, it has been a challenge for me over the years and I know that I must be deliberate if I am to stick to my own schedule.

Pragmatic Point: Avoid the "long no" when you need to give someone an answer.

In addition to your own, personal time management skills, it's important to respect other people's time. People who give you focused time and attention and get back to you with a polite and timely "no," are far better for your personal cause than those who string you along because they don't want to hurt your feelings. Be just as considerate with others and learn to firmly, but politely, say "no" when you need to and do so in a timely and respectful manner. Perhaps you can suggest someone who might be able to help them.

Remember to take **C.H.A.R.G.E.** of your life. Time is too valuable and learning this skill gives you and others more quality time to spend on people and projects that are of real value to you and others.

"Tell me yes, tell me no, just PLEASE tell me!" **Rocco Petrelli, Managing Partner PRIMA Business Specialists**

How good are you at managing your time? If you're lacking in this area, you can read more about time management on my website. I've compiled a list of articles to give you further assistance on this matter. You can find those resources here: PragmaticPassion.com/bookresources.

Objective 3: Passion, Persistence, and Perseverance Matter

The 8 P's of Perseverance: *"Pursue your Purpose with Passionate Persistence; Pivot if Prudent; and Patiently Persevere."*

Achieving personal and professional success is not an easy task that happens quickly, whimsically, or without sacrifice. Oh yes, there are rare occasions when overnight successes occur, but just like the "one hit wonders" in the music industry, the glory is fleeting and in most cases, unsustainable.

You may recognize these familiar sayings about persistence and perseverance:

- "Winners never quit and quitters never win."

- "Success is falling nine times and getting up ten."

- "Never give up. Never surrender!"

- And this classic from baseball legend Yogi Berra, "It ain't over 'til it's over."

Sacrifice and perseverance pay off with four consecutive ACHA National Championships.

As a coach, I believed in having a theme for every season and sometimes those themes became a permanent part of the team culture going forward. For example, "Expect to Win!" was about having the confidence and believing we could get over the hump against an arch-nemesis. Because we changed our mindset, we had the confidence to go out and do it on the ice. "Good is the Enemy of Excellent" was about battling complacency and pushing ourselves to become our very best as we were going for our fourth consecutive ACHA National Championship in 2003.

But my favorite theme remains, "Champions Find A Way." Even though our 1999-2000 team included 13 freshmen, we won three come-from-behind overtime games in a row en route to an improbable ACHA National Championship. Talk about perseverance and never giving up! Those players were amazing. In fact, that group of freshmen went on to win four consecutive National Championships, in four very different ways (great goaltending, a powerful offense, a balanced attack, and grinding it out).

There may be times when you feel like giving up along your journey, and having a personal theme or mantra that aligns with your goals can help you through those tough times. Passion combined with persistence allows you to persevere.

Passion Point: Having a personal "theme" that you can focus on each day is a great way to provide positive daily affirmation.

Real Life 101 – WETSU!

When I was a young counselor, coach, and instructor at Culver Military Academy, I had a senior cadet in my unit, Battery "C," named Rick Rosemark. Our unit had its backs against the wall preparing the barracks for the Annual Formal Inspection and I expressed concerns over the difficulties we would face and whether the unit was capable of persevering.

I have never forgotten Rick's response. He said, "No problem Mr. B, WETSU!" I said, "WETSU?" Rick replied with a confident grin, "We Eat That S#!t Up!"

Talk about a "can-do attitude!" I am not surprised that today Rick is the owner of his own telecommunications business, Ricktel Communications in New England. To this day when I hear people talk about some great challenge or obstacle, I often find my inner voice saying, "WETSU!"

"Our greatest weakness lies in giving up, the most certain way to succeed is to always try just one more time." **Thomas Edison, Scientist, Inventor of the light bulb**

1. When Persistence and Perseverance Diverge

Sir Winston Churchill, Prime Minister of Great Britain during WWII and one of the greatest orators in history, is quoted most often for this saying, "Never, never, ever, give up." While he indeed has uttered those exact words, they were meant in the context of fighting for the very existence of his country. A more appropriate Churchill quote for our Pragmatic Passion purposes is:

"Never give in - never, never, never, never, in nothing great or small, large or petty, never give in EXCEPT to convictions of honor and good sense. Never yield to force; never yield to the apparently overwhelming might of the enemy."

Churchill added the very pragmatic exception that it is sometimes necessary, and practical, to cease an effort due to matters of law, honor, and common sense.

Looked at another way, "Never, never ever give up" means to keep trying and never stop working for your goals, even if you need to be flexible and pivot when you reach dead ends. There is no shame in taking one step back sometimes to gain two steps forward. Persistence, taken too far, is the equivalent of stubbornness and can lead to futility and great disappointment, even depression.

Pragmatic Point: It takes a very strong, mature person to look in the mirror and recognize their limitations.

2. Prove Them Wrong

"Never underestimate the heart of a champion" **Rudy Tomjanovich, NBA Champion Basketball Coach**

There are so many examples of individuals, businesses, and sports teams who have proven the "experts" wrong and overcome adversity with passion, persistence and perseverance. I encourage you to take time to look up these individuals online to learn more about their unlikely and amazing stories of success:

Ursula M. Burns was raised by a single mother in the projects of New York City but earned both a B.S. and M.S in engineering and became the first African American CEO of a Fortune 500 company at Xerox in 2009.

Sylvester Stallone was born in New York City's Hell's Kitchen area with paralysis that left him with a speech impediment. In his mid-20's he was homeless and broke before he wrote the script for, and starred in the lead role for, the Academy Award winning film Rocky. He went on to act, write, direct and produce over 50 major motion pictures.

Mary Barra, the daughter of a General Motors machinist, earned an engineering degree and became Chairman and Chief Executive Officer of General Motors, the first female CEO of a major global automaker.

Terry Pegula borrowed $7,500 from his mother and some friends in 1983 to start East Resources, Inc., an independent oil and gas exploration and development company, and sold the company in 2010 for $4.7 billion. Along with his wife Kim, Terry became owner of the Buffalo Bills and Buffalo Sabres, and one of the most generous philanthropists in the country.

J.K. Rowling went from poverty to international success as the author of the Harry Potter books, which have sold more than 400 million copies worldwide and have been made into seven feature films.

General Colin Powell, born in Harlem, the son of Jamaican immigrants, rose from being a "C" student to become the first Afro-Caribbean American to serve as Secretary of State, Chairman of the Joint Chiefs of Staff, and a Four Star General. A 35-year Army veteran, he received the Presidential Medal of Freedom in 1991.

Joy Mangano, a single mother of three children, who went from being a waitress to becoming a famous inventor and president of Ingenious Designs, and appearing regularly on the Home Shopping Network. She is the author of *Inventing Joy* and the 2015 film *Joy*, which was loosely based on her life.

Herb Brooks, who went from being the last player cut from the USA hockey team for the 1960 Olympics, to Gold Medal winning Head Coach of the 1980 U.S. Olympic Hockey team that inspired the movie *Miracle*. The U.S. victory over the former Soviet Union Olympic team is considered the greatest upset in sports history.

These individuals show us the importance of the right attitude, work ethic, and perseverance, and why a person's intuition, passion, and determination, not just intelligence or innate talent, are critically important.

You can make up a lot of ground for any perceived lack of talent when you simply out work others. My father, another

Passioneer, has coached baseball and softball for over 50 years. One of his favorite sayings to his players, including when he coached my brother and me was, "Hustle is a difference maker. You can make up for talent if you just outwork the other team."

There will inevitably be naysayers in your life that will just plain anger you enough that you will be driven to prove them wrong. Perhaps they were put into your life precisely for that reason and just when you needed a "wake up call," a kick in the butt, or to regain your focus. So look at them as a blessing and as a motivator.

Passion Point: Pardon my persistence in pointing out the importance of hard work, sacrifice, and discipline. I am passionate about making a difference in your life. I love helping you create dreams aligned with your purpose. You have to remember your purpose so you can keep going when life gets tough.

Real Life 101: Never Give Up!

"Our greatest glory is not in never falling but in rising every time we fall." **Confucius**

This story is about a real hero in my life, named Matt Seybert, who twice faced death before his 13th birthday, and never gave up. Neither did his family, friends, or his adopted teammates on the Penn State Hockey team.

Matt was a 9-year-old youth soccer player who suddenly began to feel weak and sick. On February 12, 2001, Matt's life changed forever when he was diagnosed with Acute Lymphoblastic Leukemia (ALL). His parents Ron and Jill were initially in a state of shock.

When his oncologist, Dr. Melanie Comito, told 9-year-old Matt what cancer was and what he would face, his reaction was priceless: "OK, well then let's do this!" Matt, a big *Star Wars* fan, drew a picture of an X-wing fighter battling an

Front row (L to R): Matt Seybert, Sarah Seybert.
Back row (L to R): Coach B, Josh Mandel, Ron Seybert,
Jill Seybert, Jamie Miller-Shipon, Paul Crooker
[*Photo Courtesy of Jay Horgas*]

Imperial Cruiser with cancer cells drawn on it. How's *that* for a positive attitude and courage!

The sacrifices Matt and his family had to endure as he began chemotherapy were significant. There was nausea, head-aches, sore muscles, hair loss, missed school, missed work, not to mention the serious stress on everyone's emotions.

A few weeks later Matt met Penn State Hockey player, Josh Mandel, through classmate and friend, Jamie Miller-Shipon. Jamie was a volunteer for Penn State's annual 46-hour stu-dent dance marathon. Known simply as THON, it is the larg-est student run philanthropy in the world and has raised al-most $150 million since 1973 for The Four Diamonds Fund to fight pediatric cancer. Matt's father Ron attended THON a few weeks after Matt's diagnosis and has not missed one since.

Matt and his family became close to many of the Icer players including Josh, Brendan and Dustin Martin, Curtiss Patrick, Brandon Cook, and especially Paul Crooker. Matt was a reg-ular at Icer hockey games, a stick boy, honorary captain (he would come on the bench during warm-ups) and was a fre-quent visitor in our locker room as a member of our team. He was an inspiration to us all.

Matt's cancer went into remission and he seemed to be doing well. But in the fall of 2002, with Matt now 11 years old, his cancer returned, and the odds of recovery dropped sharply. Matt was pretty dejected because he was very aware of what sacrifices he would have to make and the even harder challenges he was about to face.

We stopped by the house where Matt and his parents stayed in Hershey, PA during his treatments, with our team bus on the way back from a road game. The neighbors gave us some pretty funny looks when the whole team got off the bus.

The guys played video games with Matt and hung out all afternoon with the Seybert family. The team literally didn't want to head back to campus because the guys wanted to be with their "teammate." Matt's condition had gotten much worse and our visit lifted his spirits tremendously.

Matt's parents, Ron and Jill, will tell you that the Penn State ice hockey players were heroes to Matt and that the guys helped him through his battles with cancer. Well, that may be true, but I can tell you without a doubt, that Matt was an even bigger hero to our team. He was an integral part of the national championships that we won from 2001-2003. He was an inspiration to us throughout our title runs.

Matt's parents and his sister, Sarah, are heroes as well. I remember his dad Ron shaving his head when Matt's hair fell out during his chemo treatments, so Matt would feel at ease. Jill stayed at home to help care for Matt and keep the family affairs in order. Everyone had to make sacrifices. Sister Sarah was a real unsung hero, as she had to make a lot of personal sacrifices while her parents looked after Matt.

Matt's health began to return, and he was able to attend our game with St. Louis University. We were unexpectedly down 1-0 after the first period and being badly outplayed in our rink. I came in to the locker room ready to rip into the team. I yelled at everyone to sit down and be quiet. I spotted Matt sitting in the room lecturing a few of our guys. He could tell I was angry, so he got up and said he'd wait outside. On his way out though, he handed me a note with some ideas for what we needed to do. It said:

1. Get on goalies nerves
2. Keep the puck in there blue zone
3. No penalties!
4. Keep up the checking
5. Shoot More!

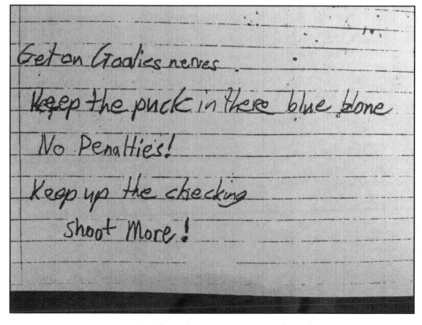

Young Matt Seybert's instructions for the team
at the end of the first period.

As I read the note, I had tears in my eyes. I took a deep breath and composed myself, and instead of lashing out at the team, I pulled out Matt's note and read it very calmly, but firmly, to the guys.

When I was done I simply said, "Can you guys do that?" The reply was an enthusiastic "YES!" As they came together at the center of the locker room I said, "The list I just read came from Matty. Do you think you can go out and do what he asks?" We stormed out of the locker room and scored 6 unanswered goals that period, en route to a 9-1 victory.

In February of 2007, I was asked to give the pre-dance pep talk that occurs just moments before the official start of THON. Standing up on stage at the Bryce Jordan Center by yourself in front of close to 10,000 dancers and supporters with a bright spotlight on you can be a bit intimidating. It was the easiest speech I ever had to give.

I began with a description of how a young boy had come to mean something special to the hockey team and me. While people looked up to our team as heroes, this young man was our hero. I described what Matt had been through and I relayed the locker room story that inspired our comeback win over St. Louis.

So, when it came time to bring Matt out on stage (wearing his Penn State Icer jersey, I might add), he sprinted toward me, and unrehearsed, jumped into my arms and hugged me with all his strength.

There wasn't a dry eye in the house as my heart raced and I felt an incredible rush of adrenaline. A 15-year-old Matt grabbed that microphone and, completely un-phased by the size of the crowd, gave one of the most inspirational speeches you can imagine. I stood there with tears of pure joy running down my cheeks.

Matt went on to earn a degree in Computer Science, has been cancer free since 2004, and is doing incredibly well, working in the technology industry as a web designer for HigherEdJobs.com.

In October of 2017, Matt proposed to his girlfriend Shelby Caraway, a "missionary kid" who has traveled the world herself in service of others. Matt asked me to be a member of their wedding party and on June 9, 2018, I was honored to serve as a groomsman in their amazing outdoor wedding that was full of joy and love.

Matt is the definition of a positive attitude, sacrifice, and courage, and why passion, persistence, and perseverance matter. He is my hero!

As my good friend Lt. Colonel Dick Bartolomea would remind me during difficult times: "Coach, when you are going through hell…just keep on going."

Chapter 3 Summary:

1. To use "The Power of Focus"

2. To manage your time. Say a polite "No" so you can get to your "Yes"

3. Passion, Persistence, and Perseverance Matter

You know you must sacrifice in order to achieve any meaningful goal in pursuit of your dreams. **Respond to these questions and statements to consider what strategies you will use to stay focused and to persevere during your journey:**

1. What personal "theme" or "mantra" can you think of that will help you stay focused and provide you with a positive daily affirmation?

_____

_____

_____

2. Think of a time when you had the strength to say "no" to a short term, impulsive decision that allowed you to stay focused on a goal.

_____

_____

_____

3. Have you ever felt that you were really busy doing work but weren't making any progress? What would you do differently the next time you are given such a task?

_____

_____

_____

4. Name a time when you were so engaged in an activity that you experienced a "state of flow."

_____

_____

_____

5. Give examples of times when you made smart choices that would be considered delayed gratification.

_____

_____

_____

6. Discuss some time management strategies that you have used effectively to keep your focus.

_____

_____

_____

7. Name a time when you persevered even though you considered giving up.

_____

_____

_____

"A dream doesn't become reality through magic; it takes sweat, determination and hard work." **General Colin Powell, Former Secretary of State**

Chapter 4
Servant Leadership

"The servant-leader is servant first... It begins with the natural feeling that one wants to serve, to serve first. Then conscious choice brings one to aspire to lead. That person is sharply different from one who is leader first."

**Robert K. Greenleaf, Founder of
The Servant-Leadership Philosophy**

Chapter 4 Objectives:

1. Someone has to **C.A.R.E.**!

2. Conflict Resolution and Feedback

3. Pragmatic Leadership

Leadership matters. We are all leaders in some way (even if it's just the leadership of YOU). It does not matter how old you are or whether you are a student or a CEO. Having a service mindset will serve you well regardless of your position or status as a student, employee, or executive.

Pragmatic Point: Before you take on any leadership role, you must first serve others.

You must serve before you can lead. Let me repeat that. You MUST serve before you can lead. Being "other-centered" and keeping the "greater good" at the center of your thought process helps you to live a more prosperous and fulfilling life. Creating and providing value to others is paramount to achieving success in your personal and professional life. Having the right customer service mindset must go hand in hand with your other positive attitudes and values.

The Emmy Award winning reality TV show *Undercover Boss* (which started in 2010), really resonated with workers around the country who saw in many of the employees as kindred spirits. While watching the show many of us looked favorably at the real-life circumstances and the eye-opening epiphanies of the CEOs about how the frontline and back of house staff were being treated. The lesson here is that everybody matters and how you treat others is critical to your success.

Surround yourself with people who share a "serve others first" mentality. Work for them, hire them when you are able, support and nurture them, have them as friends, and remind yourself often that you must be one of them. We need more people who are not only driven by results, but who factor in positive treatment of others as an outcome.

Objective 1: Someone Has to C.A.R.E.!

"Nobody cares how much you know, until they know how much you care." **President Theodore Roosevelt**

When I was 11 years old I was watching a movie on TV with my father called *The Hospital* starring Academy Award winner George C. Scott. It was a satire about a Dr. Bock, the hospital administrator who attempts to cope with both his personal and professional lives unraveling simultaneously. In the final scene, Dr. Bock is preparing to run off with his girlfriend to Mexico and put all his troubles behind him. At the last moment he decides to stay behind and go back to help fix the chaos at the hospital.

As a young kid I did not understand why this hospital administrator would choose to stay instead of putting all his personal pain and professional stresses behind him. I asked my father and I have never forgotten his answer. He said, "Because someone has to care." It was a powerful moment in my life as my father explained that there are times when a leader must make personal sacrifices for the greater good.

1. Compassionate, Altruistic, Responsible, and Engaged

I created the C.A.R.E. acronym for you to remember the deeper meaning of caring for others as you search for your own purpose in life. I firmly believe that if you make helping others a priority, and a foundational skill, it will come back to you in positive ways you cannot imagine and will possibly happen when you least expect it...quite often when you need it the most.

Compassionate
Altruistic
Responsible
Engaged

Compassionate leaders have the desire to intervene and help relieve the trauma when someone, or some group, is in a state of physical or mental anguish. Compassion takes the emotional aspect of empathy and "actualizes" it. You don't simply feel another person's pain; you act on alleviating it.

Altruistic leaders are selfless, generous, and committed to helping others first and being committed to a superior effort for "The Good of The Order."

Responsible leaders have "the buck stops here" attitude and accept responsibility when events happen on their watch, even if the action was not specifically of their doing. You want to be a "stand up leader" that is willing to admit when a mistake is made and solve it rather than avoid or ignore the situation.

Engaged leaders do not just react to problems that occur and fix them, but are deeply and genuinely involved in all aspects of their role. This allows them to anticipate issues and take preventative measures to minimize any impacts from them. They also follow up on issues and help their people grow from adversity.

Passion Point: It is my hope that when I pass away, one of the things that people will say about me was that I cared. In fact, I have often told my closest friends and family that on my tombstone it would be an affirmation of a life well lived if it simply said, "He cared." I hope that you will become a more kind and caring person as a result of your Pragmatic Passion experience.

2. Teamwork

"Success is a team sport. Success takes the help of others."
Simon Sinek, Best-selling Author of Start With Why

Your ability to work with others is critical to your personal and professional success. People who can work with, and lead others, will always be in demand.

Having said that, I have a very interesting question for you. Is there an "I" in team? You bet there is and anyone who doesn't believe that self-preservation occurs, especially during times of stress, is kidding himself or herself. It makes **pragmatic** sense to look out for your self *under certain circumstances*. I still believe strongly that you must keep your ego under control, but we all, including you, have some ego within. Just keep it real!

WIIFM, or "What's in it for ME?" is absolutely a fair question. But it is fair only in the right context, and with the proper demeanor, so you are not perceived as greedy or unconcerned for others. For example, you should be paid a fair wage for your work and you must guard against being taken advantage of by educating yourself in what a fair wage means within your industry and vocation.

As a coach it would be considered blasphemy to my traditionalist friends to suggest the possibility of an "I" in team. But I want you to consider a different way of looking at the make-up of a team (or family). I want you to think outside the box and challenge the conventional wisdom once again. I want you to consider that teams are made up of unique individuals who bring different skills and strengths to the group.

1. Take care of YOU - first.

While this may at first appear selfish, it makes perfect sense in most cases because you are no good to others if you are not taking care of your own mental, physical, and spiritual wellbeing. Consider the example of airline travel, where they tell you to put the oxygen mask on yourself before helping others in the case of an emergency. Of course, there are certain times of desperation when you will make an ultimate sacrifice to save a loved one or to stand up for a belief, even though it costs you personally. But most times you will get more done, make more progress, and help more people when you first take care of yourself.

2. Take care of your family, teammates, and staff.

If you do a good job of caring for your family, your teammates, and your employees, then they are much more likely to be there for you and your customers.

3. Take care of your customers and guests.

While this may also seem backward to you, I hope you understand the reason why it is actually third. Common sense dictates that if you are at your best and that you have taken good care of your people, they will be in a much better mindset and better prepared to provide superior service and care of your customers and guests. Happy employees mean happy customers.

There are several counterintuitive books on this subject, including *The "I" in Team* by John J. Murphy and Michael McMillan. They believe there are many I's in team ranging from interdependence, inspiration, intelligence, intuition, ingenuity, integrity, and influence.

Teamwork is really "connected independence" which is simply recognizing that it is the unique skills and strengths that individuals bring that make us stronger as an interdependent team.

"No accomplishment of real value has ever been achieved by a human being working alone." **John Maxwell, Best Selling Author and Speaker**

My good friend Marty Wolff, host of *The Business Builders Show* on The C-Suite Network, interviewed Bob Chapman, CEO of Barry-Wehmiller, a global provider of manufacturing technology. Bob talked about his best-selling book *Everybody MATTERS! The Extraordinary Power of Caring for Your People Like Family*. At his company, Bob says, "We measure success by the way we touch the lives of people." Which is why they are consistently ranked among the top places to work because employees feel they are truly supported and work in a caring, family environment.

> **Passion Point:** The almost indescribable, awesome feelings of high achievement are saved for those whose collaborative efforts create positive impact for the greater good.

From my perspective, there is nothing like the exhilaration of winning a team championship or celebrating the launch of a new product with your colleagues. Those accomplishments can be achieved only with a high level of teamwork, and the ability to set aside your ego for the greater good. This is essential for any successful servant leader.

"It's amazing what you can accomplish when you do not care who gets the credit." **President Harry Truman**

Objective 2: Conflict Resolution and Feedback

"There is a 'win-win' solution to just about everything when you start with good intentions." **Joe Battista**

Inevitably there will be disagreements and conflict in both your personal and professional lives. It is critical to learn how to debate without being debatable, and I am talking about debating in-person, using verbal discourse, and not texting or tweeting one another where you lose demeanor, inflection, and context of the message.

Successful "win-win" conflict resolution occurs when we understand the power of empathy by walking in another person's shoes and we allow for context and perspective. You should assume in many cases that "you probably know half the story at best." Trust, but verify your sources and use your intuition and your critical thinking skills before jumping to conclusions. I have personally made this mistake far too many times, especially when speed, and not accuracy, is all the rage in social media.

Focus on arriving at good choices and decisions that are far more likely to occur when egos have been "checked at the door" and a feeling of psychological safety exists. That is often up to you to lead by example in your role as a servant leader.

It takes only one person to create a conflict. Identification of it, and respectful communication with the other person(s) is an essential first step to resolution. Own your piece, and ask the other person to own theirs. Finish with a plan to prevent the same conflict from happening again. Conflict resolution is a little-known art in business and personal lives. Spend deliberate time learning this skill.

"The distance between debate and resolution is where you find compromise." **R.J. Stasieczko, Intra-Entrepreneur**

1. Initiate the "C.H.E.C.K." Response

While it is popular to come to the conclusion to "agree to disagree, without being disagreeable," I believe too often this is simply a cop out. This rarely resolves anything and simply results in "kicking the can down the road" so it becomes someone else's problem in the future. Hence, my personal disdain for those politicians and bureaucrats who are survivalists. In too many cases they sacrifice having the tough conversations and negotiating a pragmatic resolution for the greater good, while simply trying to keep their jobs.

What ever happened to good old-fashioned civil and respectful debate and discussion? My belief is that you always want to get the right people around the right table and be comfortable enough to be transparent, especially when the decision is going to impact so many.

When a disagreement arises with a customer or colleague, pause, take a deep breath, and initiate the "C.H.E.C.K." response: – Use **C**ivility, **H**umor, **E**mpathy, **C**ooperation, and **K**indness.

Civility - Treat the other person(s) politely and respectfully with the intent of a positive outcome.

Humor - If appropriate, interject some humor to defuse the situation.

Empathy - Walk in the other person's shoes, see their perspective, and listen compassionately.

Cooperation - Try to find a "win-win" solution and negotiate an acceptable conclusion.

Kindness - Treat people with dignity and grace even if things don't work out. Always take the high road.

Passion Point: Humor can sometimes defuse tense situations. For example, in describing empathy to a group of coaches, I once heard a colleague say, "Empathy is about walking a mile in another person's shoes. Feel what they feel. Besides, if you still disagree, you are a mile away from them...and you have their shoes!"

2. Feedback is a Blessing.

Michael Josephson, Founder of The Josephson Institute of Ethics, says, "You don't have to be sick to get better." I have used this quote throughout my time as a coach, administrator, and speaker to emphasize the importance of having a growth mindset and to guard against complacency.

Success in business, at work, in sports, and in personal achievements can at times mask subtle flaws that if not corrected, could lead to long-term issues. If we are not purposely seeking candid, but helpful debriefs and feedback, then we are not growing. Sometimes success is serendipitous. You'll take it, but it would serve you well to ask the probing questions that allow for sustainable success going forward.

Researchers at Harvard showed that the vast majority of us believe in feedback. After all, don't you want to know you are doing great, or at least okay? They also found that most people dread giving and receiving feedback for fear of confrontation or conflict if the news is not delivered or received well.

In a 2013 *Harvard Business Review* research study asked, "What do employees want most from a supervisor?" The number one response was to "feel valued and respected."

"SHOUT PRAISE!...Whisper criticism." **Chuck Daley, coach of America's Gold Medal "Dream Team" in Olympic Basketball in 1992**

I firmly believe that feedback is a true blessing. Even if it's sometimes wrong! We can still learn something from every attempt to evaluate our performance, even if we don't agree with it or don't particularly care for the person delivering the message.

Navy Seals are legendary for their use of "After Action Reports" (AAR) in which everyone can be vulnerable while feeling the psychological safety to be candid. When a Special Forces team member makes a mistake, it can cost a teammate their life. While we are rarely in life and death decision making situations, a lot can be learned from being confident enough to have brutally honest discussions.

"Am I therefore your enemy, because I tell you the truth?" **The Bible, King James Version (KJV), Galatians 4:16**

I want to reiterate the importance of getting the right people, around the right table, able to talk openly and candidly about the toughest subjects without fear of retribution. This is critical to real success. Don't surround yourself with "yes" people who give you the bobble-head response you want to hear. There is a big difference between a "naysayer" and a "truth teller." A mentor, who is telling you what you need to hear even if you don't want to hear it, is trying to help you grow.

They may have recognized some character flaw or habit that is holding you back and usually have some advice on how to overcome it. The naysayer is simply a negative, cynical, and often-jealous and toxic person you need to avoid.

Delivering and receiving corrective feedback is one of the hardest aspects of leadership and a servant leader will do everything possible to deliver, or receive, feedback with empathy, grace, and dignity in order to be effective.

When I coached, we talked to our team captains about snuffing out "Bitcher's Corner." It's where players who might not be in the line-up or playing as much as they (or their parents) believed they should gathered in small groups to complain. It's the group that bashes others on social media but won't confront the people face to face. It took me time to realize it, and to have the confidence to nip that negativity in the bud before it became a cancer. Positivity almost always beats negativity, especially in school, work, and at home.

Consider these two ways a leader can handle a suggestion from a group member:

1. "That's a terrible idea. We'd be stretching our existing staff too far. Dumbest thing I have ever heard!"

2. "Good input. For me to get behind this idea, I'd need to know that we could properly staff this without sacrificing quality."

Number one is judgmental, personal, and rude. How would you feel if you were on the receiving end of that rant? The second response is nurturing and supportive and clearly lays out an expectation for a next step.

It is critically important to train leaders how to deliver timely feedback. It is also important to go to great lengths to properly train anyone tasked with delivering a performance review. There are few more difficult functions in leadership roles than getting this highly personal interaction right.

I doubt that very many organizations or families take the time for this crucial part of any successful relationship. Great leaders, true friends, and caring family members will use "tough love" and sometimes tell you what you don't want to hear. Even when it is well meaning, spot on, and intended to help you to improve, you might get defensive and start tuning out their message while you already started to organize your response in your head! Have you ever done that? I know I have, and it usually ends poorly and at a minimum, with a lost opportunity to grow.

The sooner you learn to "get over yourself" and accept feedback, the sooner you will embrace a growth mindset and begin improving. I am sure you have heard the phrase "the best lessons in life were usually the hardest." It took someone to have the courage to look you in the eye and tell you what you needed to hear. Be a coach and be coachable.

Pragmatic Point: While it is critical to learn how to deliver constructive "teachable moments," it is equally important to learn *how to receive* candid, meaningful, and growth-oriented feedback.

Objective 3: Pragmatic Leadership

"Real leadership is about building other people and shining your light on them, not on yourself." **John Addison, Author, Former CEO of Primerica**

Leadership is one of the most studied and discussed qualities in human existence. There are hundreds of definitions, tons of books, videos, webinars, and seminars available on every type of leadership derivative you can imagine (but we will continue to find more I am sure!).

At its core, real leadership is not a title or a position, although traditionally it has often been looked at this way. It's certainly not just management or supervision, as there are very successful managers and supervisors who are not effective leaders. It's definitely not just someone standing in front of a group and giving a rah-rah speech or showing a pump-up video. I can do that in my sleep and so can many others. Its impact is typically fleeting and better left for the locker room.

"The key to successful leadership today is influence, not authority." **Dr. Ken Blanchard, Best-selling Author and Management Expert.**

Pragmatic leaders use influence and persuasion with a positive intent to have others do what needs to be done without using fear tactics. Do not, however, confuse influence and persuasion with manipulation. Manipulation is a negative aspect of leadership focused on power and control and is self-serving.

1. The Price of Leadership

"Courage is what it takes to stand up and speak; courage is also what it takes to sit down and listen." **Sir Winston Churchill**

If I had to boil leadership down to one simple quality, for me it would be this: **Courage.**

Regardless of the situation or circumstances, ultimately a leader must have the courage to act when necessary, the courage to remain patient when it's prudent, and the courage to make difficult decisions, even if unpopular. The best leaders I know are confident enough to accept responsibility for their decisions, right or wrong, regardless of whether there may be substantial criticism. That is the price of leadership. It is a skill that you can and must learn and become very comfortable in demonstrating over and over to make a positive difference in a variety of situations.

It may be tougher today to be a leader due to social media scrutiny of every decision. While a great person may make thousands of good decisions and choices in the face of enormous pressure, we tend to be a society that remembers the few, or even just one, negative. Resist this temptation with all your heart and soul and be a forgiveness practitioner. A person is much more than their mistakes, even the costliest ones.

We have far too many managers who are survivalists at their jobs (likely one of the 51% that Gallup says "...are just there"). Real leadership takes courage and fortitude.

We are all leaders in some form. You may someday be the head of a company, chairperson of a committee, coach of a youth sports team, head of a household, or the president of a volunteer board. At a bare minimum you are the leader of yourself. While speaking at a Sports Business Conference in March of 2018, a former Hockey Management Association member, Justin Charschan (now with Major League Baseball Advanced Media), mentioned to the audience that, "Coach Battista would often tell our students to **be the CEO of you**." It's always good to know that your message is being heard and applied.

We live at a most remarkable time in human history, with more information and the ability to connect with billions of people with just the push of a few buttons. It is an exciting time full of opportunity and technological advances. However, there are also unintended consequences as we innovate and change. This is also the "Age of Rage," "Fake News," and the time of "Critics Without Credentials" that dominate our social media driven world. Learning how to cope with and resolve conflict will save you from anxiety, depression, anger, and other time-wasting health issues that you can control with a great attitude and the courage to do the right things when needed.

As a USA Hockey Coaches Instructor, I frequently give a talk about preparing a team to be champions at playoff time. Not just winning, but winning championships. There is a big difference. It actually starts at the very beginning of every new season, the start of a new school year, or the start of a new fiscal year in business. A lot of teams/organizations have talent and even great coaching/management. Championship teams (and organizations) have team chemistry and courageous leadership.

Passion Point: When I was coaching, I resolutely believed that if I could give a team two qualities at the beginning of each season, it would be these: great leadership and team chemistry.

2. The Margin of Excellence

"Good is the Enemy of Excellence" **Jim Collins, Author of Good to Great**

When we think of a "margin of excellence" it often refers to making a difference in fundraising efforts or increasing profit margins in business. I want you look at it in a new way as a measure of the courage it takes to make great decisions.

What is my take on "the margin of excellence"?

At the margin, at the moment of a critical decision point when the pressure is on, what will you, as a leader, manager, employee, parent, or friend do to be a positive difference maker? Will you have the COURAGE to make the tough calls at the "moments of truth"? They occur multiple times every day, sometimes subtly; sometimes they come crashing down on top of you!

There will come a time in your life when you must make a stand. It could be a decision impacting your family, your career, your finances, your health, etc. More importantly, it could greatly impact others who are affected by your action or inaction.

Will YOU be a courageous person and servant leader **at that very moment**? We have already discussed the fact that it is easy to lead when all is well. We know it's easy to be a critic, a skeptic, cynical and sarcastic when others are faced with tough choices in adverse conditions. But how will you respond?

Well, I sincerely hope that from what you are learning in this book, that you will not make any rash or irrational decisions. You cannot "just do it" or "go for it" based solely on emotion and societal pressure. You must apply your Pragmatic Passion vision and purpose and use common sense as your guide. Trust in yourself and what you have learned. Use your skills and knowledge to formulate the proper response or decision.

Then, once you have made your choice, "Get It Done!"

If you are a real servant leader, you will step in and stop someone from bullying or belittling others. You will speak up in a meeting and go against the conventional wisdom in the room to share your opinion on a divisive and critically important topic, with poise and grace. If you make a mistake, which you will at times, you will own it and move forward while acknowledging and learning from it.

Real Life 101: Applying the Margin of Excellence: Part One

We all face critical times in our lives. Personally, I have had a few and can attest that when I stood up for what I believed in, for what aligned with my passion and my purpose, it was worth it. Even if the stance I took led to negative reactions and even consequences from those who disagreed with me at the time. There was a particularly tense meeting that took place during the construction of Pegula Ice Arena at Penn State in May of 2013 where one such moment presented itself. I knew what I wanted to say regarding a significant budgetary decision and knew it would be controversial.

I was holding my tongue with all my might until the project manager, Steve Laurila, asked for my opinion. I was put on the spot and you could hear a pin drop in the crowded conference room. I can tell you it would have been much easier to give a "bobble head" answer at that moment. All that went through my mind in that moment was how many times I have given the talk to others on having the courage to do what must be done **at the margin, at that moment**, to make all the difference. I gave an impassioned opinion on why I believed we needed to keep a few specific amenities in the building and we owed it to our generous donors, the Pegulas, to do so.

After a brief discussion it was clear there was now overwhelming support to follow my recommendation. It was difficult, but worth it, and every time I am in the arena I realize it was the right thing to do. I have certainly made my share of poor decisions and have spoken out of turn during my career. But in that moment, in part because of lessons learned, and because it aligned with my passion and my purpose, it was also the pragmatic action to take. At that moment, the decision to take a stand created a margin of excellence.

3. The Servant Leader Pre-Decision Checklist

As a servant leader you need to ask yourself these questions before you make tough decisions:

- Is it morally correct?

- Is it ethically correct?

- Is it legal?

- Is it safe?

- Is it the right thing to do?

- Does it pass the "Front Page" and "Social Media Trending" Test? (i.e. media scrutiny)

These may seem like common sense questions, but I have found that common sense is not as common as you would believe. We all need reminders that our actions have consequences.

Having said that, there are certain times as a leader when it is necessary to challenge the status quo, to avoid the "sea of sameness," to forget playing it safe, and to go above and beyond compliance. Especially when it's the right thing to do. Most policies and procedures are guidelines. As long as your alternative solution passes the "Servant Leader Pre-Decision Checklist," there may come a time when you have to do what must be done.

Don't just think outside the box, have the courage to get rid of the box - to allow yourself and your team to use intuition, ingenuity, and critical thinking skills to make a tough judgment call. That is a key difference between a leader and a manager, and it is my strong belief that we need more real leaders now than ever before.

Pragmatic Point: Beware the "Agenda Zombies" not savvy enough to be willing to adjust during a critical moment in a meeting simply for the sake of sticking to an arbitrary agenda.

Have you ever been in a meeting and right when your group is about to make a game changing major breakthrough on a big priority, the "manager" mindset sometimes overrides the "leader" mindset. The manager tells everyone, "We need to stick to the agenda!" A missed opportunity occurs because the "Agenda Zombie" intervened and instead of being a real leader and making an adjustment to the meeting, a significant new idea or tough decision may be glossed over. There are weak-minded managers who are more determined to get to that least important item on the agenda, so they can simply check it off!

The best leaders recognize that agendas are necessary, but so is flexibility, especially at critical times. That is the difference "at the margin" between a leader and a manager.

Real Life 101: Applying the Margin of Excellence: Part Two

One of the worst customer service debacles ever took place in April 2017 on a United Airlines Flight when a video went viral of a bloodied passenger literally being dragged off a United Airlines plane for a procedural issue that could have easily been handled well with some leadership and critical thinking skills. The airline suffered significant brand damage and its stock price plummeted.

In his article entitled "United Airlines and the Fiduciary Paradox: Providing a Margin of Excellence," guest columnist Don Trone, former director of the Institute for Leadership at the U.S. Coast Guard Academy, wrote the following:

> Consider the United Airlines incident this week when a passenger was dragged off of an overbooked flight. The website www.askthepilot.com has provided the most plausible explanation as to why the United staff failed to act in the best interests of its customers:
>
> "Everything is scripted and rote and procedural, and employees are often so afraid of being reprimanded for making a bad decision (not to mention being pressed for time) that they don't make a decision at all, or will gladly hand the matter to somebody else [in this case to police] who

can take responsibility. By and large, workers are deterred from thinking creatively exactly when they need to."

Passion Point: There are times, at the margin, when a real leader must find the courage to go above and beyond compliance to do the right thing even if it means pushing the limits on the interpretation of a rule, procedure, or policy. People with a growth mindset aspire to "do great things" and not be paralyzed by a "just don't do anything wrong" mentality.

As a Servant Leader:

- Do not be afraid to make decisions…or mistakes.

- Check your ego at the door and show humility.

- Have the courage to get yourself out of your comfort zone.

- Encourage people to step out of their comfort zones.

- Be a problem preventer first, and a problem solver second!

- Be willing to improvise, adapt, and overcome adversity.

A final key concept for both superior service and servant leadership is **the importance of forgiveness**. Be able to recognize that a mistake was made, own up to it, gain wisdom from it, and move on from it. We are human, and mistakes occur. I know I have "done unto others," and others have "done unto me." Will you allow the negative energy from bitterness to stand between you and your dream? Will you be the victim or the victor?

If you are a true servant leader, you will have the courage to ask for, and grant, forgiveness. Then get past it quickly, with dignity and compassion, and get back on the right path to continue your journey. Sometimes granting forgiveness takes more courage than asking for it, especially with a team and in critical business situations.

"What to do with a mistake: recognize it, admit it, learn from it, and forget it." **Dean Smith, Hall of Fame Basketball Coach at the University of North Carolina**

4. Superior Service Leads to Business Success

Studies have shown that the benefits to working in a service-related job, especially at a young age, lead to more confidence and success down the road across many vocations. The real life experiences in dealing with people provide the best laboratory for learning how to put into practice "common courtesy and mutual respect." You will learn key skills and life lessons for achieving success that will remain with you even if you desire to be a successful CEO of a major corporation.

If you want to learn about great customer service you should study the best in the business. From my personal experiences, few organizations do it as well as Disney. Do you know who is in charge of cleaning the park at Disney properties? Everyone! If there is trash lying on the ground it doesn't matter if it's the CEO, cast members, or the actual janitorial staff, everyone at Disney pitches in so that the park is kept in spectacular shape all the time.

You are always "on," especially in this digital era. You must be prepared to give your best effort even on days when you don't feel great. It doesn't matter whether you are a student, working at a convenience store, a salesperson trying to close a big sale, the president of a large company, or a Disney character working in one of their parks. There may be days when you have low energy, may be sick, are feeling overwhelmed, dealing with a personal crisis, or your dog ran away. It does not matter. You must show your grit, be a "grinder" and find a way to work through it. *Champions find a way!*

In my part of the country, Sheetz convenience stores (family owned) have dominated a market that was once held by a competitor. They started with just one store in 1952, but due in large part to their commitment to "servant leadership" and "total customer focus," they have grown to over 500 stores in six states. They see themselves as a restaurant that sells gas and not a gas station that sells food. Their MTO (made to order) concept revolutionized the convenience store business. Their focus extends to a commitment to cleanliness, especially in their bathrooms, and safety, where as an example, they spend extra on concrete instead of asphalt (for better reflection of lighting) to brighten up their parking areas. This total commitment to customer focus has allowed Sheetz to build a very strong brand loyalty.

When it comes to serving others, you must try to go above and beyond and deliver more than you promise. If you don't take care of your customers, someone else will!

"Great leaders are almost always great simplifiers, who can cut through argument, debate, and doubt, to offer a solution everybody can understand." **Colin Powell, Retired 4-Star General and Former Secretary of State**

Chapter 4 Summary:

1. Someone has to **C.A.R.E.**!

2. Conflict Resolution and Feedback

3. Pragmatic Leadership

A Servant Leadership philosophy will not only make you a better person and leader, it will help you to achieve impactful goals in support of your purpose. **Answer these questions about what strategies you will use to better serve and to become a better leader during your journey:**

1. Describe a time in your life when you volunteered for an organization or project without any compensation.

_____

_____

_____

2. How did you feel at the conclusion of your time with the project or program?

_____

_____

_____

3. Give an example of when you or someone you know well went above and beyond expectations to help others or to add value for a client.

_____

_____

_____

4. Have you ever had a situation where it seemed like everything was unraveling before you and you still had to get somewhere for work or school? Describe what that felt like and how you may have handled it better or differently.

_____

_____

_____

5. If I asked your Pragmatic Passion Partner if you were a caring person, what would they say?

_____

_____

_____

6. When you had to deal with a difficult person at work or at home, how did you handle the situation?

_____

_____

_____

7. What character traits do you feel are the most important for leaders to be impactful?

_____

_____

_____

8. Describe a situation where you had to show courage and fortitude under pressure.

_____

_____

_____

"Leaders are also expected to work harder than those who report to them and always make sure that their needs are taken care of before yours." **Elon Musk, CEO of SpaceX and Tesla**

Chapter 5
Inspiration

"You need a team to complete your dreams."

Joe Battista

Chapter 5 Objectives:

1. Find your inspiration.

2. Surround yourself with great people who will challenge you to be better.

3. Find your mentors and coaches.

4. Find your daily motivation to live an inspired life!

You must be *inspired* to create your dreams and aspirations. You must stay motivated to achieve your goals. Both are more likely to happen when you have a great team of advisors helping you. For your part, you must be willing to ask for assistance, find resources to keep you motivated, and listen intently to those who you have chosen to be part of your own "dream team" of Pragmatic Passion Advisors.

We all need mentors and we all need coaches, just as much as we need role models and heroes. Role Models, heroes, a certain song, a great movie, an impactful speech, or some special life moment, may be the very spark that ignites a fire within you, which helps to inspire you. But to sustain the motivation to complete your dreams over the long haul, I believe you need additional support. You need a team of advisors, mentors, and coaches who genuinely care about you as an individual and sincerely want to help you to achieve success.

I challenge you to pledge to yourself that you will not spend your life living vicariously through others, whether it's a movie or TV character, a celebrity, a professional athlete, or the latest social media sensation. A super hero, a movie character, a great musician, or an athlete may inspire you, but they will only temporarily motivate you. Pragmatically, they are there primarily for entertainment value. Living out a fantasy is, in essence, a false dream and may wrongly inspire you to aim for unrealistic expectations and unachievable goals. Visualization and fantasizing are two completely different things! Visualization is the intentional and deliberate practice of seeing yourself taking action and doing the work. Fantasizing is simply hoping and wishing for something.

Pragmatic Point: You will receive incredible value by choosing a great mentor and working with a life coach or business coach who knows you and understands your Pragmatic Passion.

As we learned in Chapter 3, time is a resource that is simply too precious to squander. In our youth we rarely realize the value of our time. Who you spend time with will impact your future more than you may appreciate. So be deliberate and intentional about whom you may want as a mentor or a coach.

Objective 1: Find Your Inspiration

"Inspiration is something that you feel on the inside, while motivation is something from the outside that compels you to take action. Inspiration is a driving force, while motivation is a pulling force." **Ron Prasad, Author, Speaker, Anti-Bullying Campaigner at www.BeatBullyingWithConfidence.com**

Inspiration comes from deep within you and touches your heart and soul. You can get your inspiration from an event, from people, from your own life experiences, or from a book (hopefully this one!). Inspiration literally translates to "in spirit" and is a key part of the ancient Greek formula for *Arête*, the perfect blending of body, mind, and spirit that we learned about earlier.

A lifetime of coaching and working with others was the inspiration that fueled my burning desire to continue helping others. I was motivated to complete this book in order to launch a new career in public speaking and success coaching that could be a transformational and life changing way to help others.

Go back and look at your list of passions and your Pragmatic Passion Vision Statement. Think hard about the people and events in your life that may have inspired you in formulating your goals. Who or what inspired you to write your Pragmatic Passion Vision Statement?

When I was in the midst of my own self-doubt in college and was going through some serious soul searching, an extraordinary event inspired me beyond anything I had ever felt before. The 1980 U.S. Olympic hockey team's "Miracle on Ice" victory over the former Soviet Union team (considered the greatest assembly of hockey players ever) had a profound impact on me. It is what most sports media members still consider the greatest upset in the history of sport. The herculean effort of a group of college aged kids, most only a few years older than me at the time, inspired me to want to be a part of the growth of hockey in the U.S.A. It was the spark that inspired a change in my college career and life.

So, what inspires you? What makes you feel like you are moving toward fulfilling your aspirations? What puts you in that "state of flow" where everything feels in balance and is effortless and you simply lose track of time because you are so engaged and focused?

List the top moments, people, events, or ideas, which have inspired you in your life so far.

Here are some examples of mine:

Moments: Astronaut Neil Armstrong's first steps on the Moon, my wedding, and my kids' births.

People: Herb Brooks, Bob Johnson, David Schwartz, Harvey MacKay, and Bobby Orr.

Events: The 1980 USA Olympic Hockey Team's "Miracle on Ice"

Books: *The Magic of Thinking Big*, *The Edge*, *Good To Great*, and *Unbroken*

Movies: *Star Wars*, *Excalibur*, *Shawshank Redemption*, *Apollo 13*, and *Miracle*

Songs: "The Impossible Dream," "Rocky Theme," "Rise," and "Come Alive"

"You can live a day in your life, or put life into your day!"
Brad Killmeyer, Professional Speaker and Author of Write To Dream

Real Life 101: The Magic of Thinking BIG

"Do what you fear and fear disappears. Action Cures Fear."
Dr. David Schwartz

In 1980, as a Junior at Penn State, I had the good fortune to attend the Omicron Delta Kappa National Leadership Society (ODK) Convention in Lexington, KY as Penn State's student representative along with our faculty advisor, legendary accounting professor G.K. Nelson. To be in the same room with hundreds of the top student leaders from around the country was amazing, even more so, because I was a last minute fill-in for our organization's president, who could not make the trip. Another example of "luck favors the prepared."

Our keynote speaker was Dr. David Schwartz, author of *The Magic of Thinking BIG*. He was the most incredibly entertaining, energetic, and inspiring presenter I had ever seen in person to that point in my life. I made sure to introduce myself to him and to thank him for inspiring me to be more than I thought I could be. He was so genuine and wanted to know all about *my* aspirations! I walked away from his program with a completely new mindset and an affirmation that I *did* fit in amongst these top student leaders, even though I was not even close to being one of the smartest students in attendance! I bought his book *The Magic of Thinking BIG* and immediately read it cover to cover and still refer to it often. In fact, I have referenced it so often that it is literally held together with a binder clip.

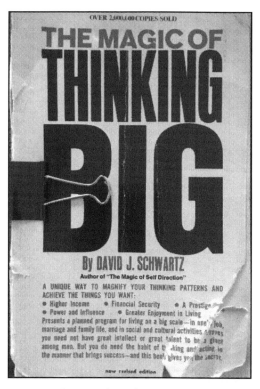

Meeting speaker and author Dr. David Schwartz
inspired me to read his book, and reading
it changed my life.

Pragmatic Point: When you attend conferences or lectures, do your best to meet the speaker and ask an intelligent question based on the material presented. If possible, find out where they are going to be later so you can either converse with them or be close enough to hear what they are talking about! Find the courage to give them your business card and contact them personally (not just ask to connect on LinkedIn!).

I have had the privilege of hearing a number of outstanding world-class speakers in person including Harvey MacKay, Jim Tunney, Patrick Lencioni, as well as Dr. David Schwartz. With all the technology available today, there is every opportunity for you to learn from some of the top leaders in business, politics, government, management, athletics, via webinars and podcasts. You just need to commit to making it a part of your daily routine.

"Motivation is when you get hold of an idea and carry it through to its conclusion, and inspiration is when an idea gets hold of you and carries you where you are intended to go." **Dr. Wayne Dyer, Author of Change Your Thoughts – Change Your Life**

Objective 2: Surround Yourself with Great People

"Surround yourself with people who will challenge you to be better." **Bob Johnson, Former Head Coach, Pittsburgh Penguins and U.S. Olympic Hockey Team**

Choose your friends and influencers wisely. Everyone wants to fit in with certain social groups and hang out with people who you believe think the way you do; that is human nature. You must do your best to develop the self-awareness to discern who are your real friends, and who stands in your way and drains energy in your life. Then, you must summon the self-confidence to respectfully separate yourself from the naysayers and negative influencers and surround yourself with the people who consistently make you better. That takes intentional and deliberate courage!

I was fortunate to have great life-long childhood friends from Penn Hills like Lou Longo, Clark Dexter, and Don Studebaker who had a shared passion for sports and academics. We had our share of fun and were never to be confused with perfect angels. But whatever trouble we got into was general mischief in nature. If you find yourself in a situation where you are surrounded by influencers who keep tempting you to make poor choices, do whatever you can to avoid them. There is no better way than to be involved in programs at school or in the community that have a positive goal.

Take a moment and think about your peers:

1. Who are the people you spend the most time with?

2. Are they a positive influence in your life?

3. Are you a good friend or colleague to them?

4. Who are the negative influencers in your life who put you down and hold you back?

Childhood friends Clark Dexter (kneeling), me,
Lou Longo, and Don Studebaker at the Penn State
Hockey Golf Outing.

Relationships are a two-way street. It's give and take and if
you want good relationships, you must give as well as receive. In their book *The PITA Principle: How to Work With
and Avoid Becoming a Pain In The Ass*, Bob Orndorf and
Dulin Clark describe two types of PITAs. The first PITA is the
"Pain In The Ass," who is difficult to deal with, unpleasant,
constantly frustrates you, and is emotionally draining. The
second PITA stands for "Professionals Increasing Their
Awareness." It describes people who have the self-awareness
to look in the mirror and realize that no one is perfect and
will work on improving their own interpersonal skills when
building and maintaining relationships. You need to aspire to
be the second kind of PITA and build better relationships at
home, at school, and at work.

You must develop and maintain the courage to move away and stay away from your toxic influencers, your "Debbie Downers" and "Negative Neds." For some of you it can be hard to recognize, realize, and reject some people in your life who may seem nice, but bring drama and a level of thinking that ultimately holds you back from pursuing your dreams. There are even people in your life who will appear to be supportive, but in reality, are just enablers who won't help you break free from your bad habits, demons, and vices. It could be as simple as a friend who pulls you away from studying or a colleague who pressures you into skipping a session at a conference or seminar.

More seriously, it could be someone who enables an alcohol, drug, or gambling addiction instead of a true friend or mentor who intervenes to help straighten you out. You want to spend your time with people who will help you grow. Avoid those who are jealous, and either aggressively or passively want to hold you back.

How do you do this, especially if you have trouble finding the courage to face your fears? By building a support team of advisors, mentors, and coaches. This is such a critical part of your personal and professional lives that even if you must spend money to get professional help, **then you must!** The professionals will help you develop the strategies and develop the confidence and courage to face your fears. You absolutely can do this if you are serious about making a positive change in your life. Learning the coping skills, and the ability to politely and professionally resist those who are obstacles to your success, is paramount for you to break through barriers and focus on the goals and dreams you have identified as important in your life. It's YOUR life and you must take charge!

"If you want to be a champion in life, then study what champions do. Learn from them, adapt to fit your skill set, and implement those lessons as a part of your daily routine." **Joe Battista**

1. Your Pragmatic Passion Advisors

All truly successful people throughout history have benefited from having a team of advisors, a circle of influencers, or a personal cabinet of those looking out for you and your best interests. They can offer assistance for you with personal, educational, work, or career matters. They are people in your life who you can call almost anytime to discuss almost any topic.

Your circle of advisors should be diverse across a spectrum of areas of expertise and personality types, so you don't create a "bobble head club" of people who always agree with you. You should consider someone who is willing to be your devil's advocate to challenge your thinking (you can even rotate this role among your advisors); you need an advocate who will be supportive and there for you in times of need; you need a visionary who will brainstorm new ideas and problem solving strategies; you need a doer who will take what the team of advisors recommends and help you act on it; you need someone who inspires you to stay the course. Of course, it's important to pick people you trust with this sensitive and confidential information.

I have had so many great advisors and influencers who have played a significant, positive role as a member of my own team of advisors. Unfortunately, some have passed away, and others have since retired, but all made significant impacts on my life at critical stages of my life. Here is a short list of some of my team of advisors:

Dr. Ray Lombra, Associate Dean and Economics Professor, Assistant Hockey Coach, Penn State University

Dr. Paul Cohen, Distinguished Professor of Industrial Engineering, North Carolina State, Hockey Faculty Advisor

Janet DeBlasio, CPA, Partner, The DeBlasio Group, Junior Penguins Hockey Team General Manager

Geoff Martha, EVP and Group President, Medtronic, Former Team Captain, Penn State Hockey

Ruth Hussey, Retired Academic Advisor, Penn State Division of Undergraduate Studies

Steve Smith, Retired Real Estate Attorney, Entrepreneur, and Philanthropist

Visit my website at PragmaticPassion.com/bookresources to find a more complete list of the various influencers in my life. Look at their job titles, Google search their backgrounds and their careers, and you will see a very diverse and well-rounded Pragmatic Passion Advisors Team and group of in-fluencers. I hope it will spark you in developing your own team of advisors.

Who is on your current Pragmatic Passion Advisors Team?

1. _____

2. _____

3. _____

4. _____

5. _____

Who would you like to add to your Advisors Team?

1. _____

2. _____

3. _____

4. _____

5. _____

Objective 3: Find Your Mentors and Coaches!

"As a long-time mentor and business advisor, I find it ironic that many look only to friends for advice. They forget that friends tell you what you want to hear, while good mentors tell you what you need to hear." **Martin Zwilling, CEO Startup Pro**

1. Find a Mentor!

Mentors can be different than coaches. Sometimes you can find one person who fills both roles. Regardless, you need to find your mentors and coaches by being proactive.

Mentors focus more on the growth of the "complete" individual (body, mind, and spirit) and can be either a part of an actual mentorship program, or in a volunteer capacity. A coach tends to focus on developing specific skills and knowledge that allow you to learn or improve certain skills usually related to a specific goal. In many cases a coach is hired for their expertise in a particular field such as speaking, music, sports, or education. The best mentors tend to be more relationship-based – they care more about you as a person, not just as a success at work or in school.

In author Tim Ferriss' book *Tribe Of Mentors*, the subtitle reads *Short Life Advice From The Best In The World*. What a brilliant idea! Interview some of the greatest minds across cultures, occupations, ages, genders, and ethnicities and share that knowledge with the world! His premise was simple: "What if I asked the 100+ most brilliant people the very questions I want answered for myself?"

Over the course of my life I have been blessed to have a number of mentors who have gone above and beyond to impact my personal and professional lives. You will always remember the special people in your life that went above and beyond and believed in you at a pivotal time. My 5th grade teacher Mr. Frank Kologie straightened out a class clown; my gym teacher and cross country Coach Bob Ford challenged me to be more than I thought possible; Mr. Jim Kelly and my academic advisor Dr. David Wilson changed my life in college and set me on a better path; my first boss Paul Steigerwald gave me a chance with the Pittsburgh Penguins that helped me pursue my passion. I was very fortunate to have a close knit and supportive family, too, and I know for some, that is not the case. It means you must be even more deliberate and determined to find mentors in the community, at school, or at work.

The partial list above and on my website cannot do justice to all the people who have influenced me in my life and career. They not only gave me wise and timely advice, but they kicked me in the butt when I needed it, put me in my place when I got overconfident, patted me on the back when I earned it, and most of all, they picked me up when I was knocked down and gave me the will to re-engage.

Having great mentors in your life will enhance both your personal and professional lives. Choose them wisely!

Real Life 101: My Mentors: The Docs and The Colonel

I want to highlight my relationships with my "go to" mentors to give you a sense of the impact that your most trusted mentors can have on you. There was little sugar coating at times and they hit me right between the eyes when I deserved it. I am a better person for having them care about me and guide me over the years.

The Docs: Surround yourself with people smarter than you!

I met Dr. Ray Lombra in 1987 in my first year of coaching at Penn State and we have been great friends ever since. Ray and his wife Bobbi essentially adopted me as part of their family when I was a young, wide-eyed, 27-year-old head coach. They have been steadfast friends through my engagement, wedding, the births of my children, vacations, the growth of Penn State Hockey, career changes, and just about every other phase of life.

Ray is passionate about seeing others strive for excellence and reach their potential. He is also candid, pragmatic, and practiced "tough love" as well as anyone I have known. Doc Lombra told me more than once, "You can't swing at every pitch. You can't be everything to every person." So many of our hockey players benefited from Ray's sage advice regarding school, careers, and life in general. Because he was perceived to be so tough, many of his students did not immediately appreciate his positive impact. I just believe he was delivering pragmatic advice!

Before making any critical decision, Ray would encourage me to take a step back, allow at least 24 hours to pass, and then take a *dispassionate* view of the circumstances and the facts. Hmm, that sounds like Pragmatic Passion in a nutshell. I wish I had followed his advice more often!

Pragmatic Point: Two of my favorite Doc Lombra sayings are: "Figure you know half the story at best." And "If we always agreed on everything, one of us wouldn't be needed!"

Dr. Paul Cohen has been a close friend and mentor since 1983. After 26 years at Penn State, he became a department head at North Carolina State University, yet we still communicate regularly. Paul and his wife Sarah are close friends who my wife and I can call on anytime for guidance and support. Doc Cohen is the consummate professional and a high performer in his field. While he has a different style than Doc Lombra, his message was almost always the same: have the facts, make decisions with emotions in check, make sure you understand the situation, and try to do the right thing.

Passion Point: Paul has a light-hearted wit that always included a funny line. When I was under stress, Paul would throw out a bit of funny sarcasm to lighten the moment. "Remember Joe, just when things seem their darkest...that is when everything goes completely to hell!"

Ray, Paul, and I regularly text, email, talk, or meet for a meal or a drink when possible, to talk about life, family, careers, and our shared passion for hockey. While we are most certainly friends, our relationships transcend friendship with a higher level of caring and support. We can talk about our deepest thoughts and lower our defenses to be vulnerable and authentic. They have been there for me again and again over the years. While it was the shared passion for Penn State Hockey that brought the Docs and me together over 30 years ago, it is the bonds of friendship and life memories that have made the relationships so meaningful. It will be impossible for me to ever repay them for their guidance, timely advice, brutally frank honesty, and their genuine concern for my family and our welfare.

It is my sincere hope that you will find such dedicated, candid, and impactful mentors in your life.

The Colonel: Gone Too Soon, But Never Forgotten

Lt. Colonel Richard "Dick" Bartolomea, "The Colonel," was my best friend in State College and a great mentor. The life lessons he taught thousands of Marines, students, campers, friends, as well as me, are too lengthy to even attempt to do it justice. Many of my mornings began with an early call from the Colonel, "Hey Coach, come on down to the Multi-Sport Complex, I got a fresh pot of coffee." When he was diagnosed with cancer, I hurt inside for months watching the cancer take away his strength and I was grief stricken when he finally succumbed in May of 2017. But I choose to remember the Colonel for his special friendship, for the days when I would bare my soul and seek his guidance over a coffee or walking nine holes on the golf course. He was a great patriot, leader, and friend, and inspired me every day to be a "hill climber, not a sock counter" and to be a good person.

Currently, I am part of a formal mentoring program with Pete Rohrer and Rod Burnham, two members of the S.C.O.R.E. Mentors organization. S.C.O.R.E. mentors are known across the country as "Counselors to America's Small Business." I meet with Pete and Rod every three weeks to discuss strategic planning, marketing, business planning, and product development. They are mentoring me on the nuances of starting a small business by passing on years of real life experience.

Real Life 101: The Gift of Mentorship

When I was a junior in college, my hockey coach Clayton John approached me about an opportunity to assist a local youth hockey player as a mentor. I had just started a new major, was an officer in both the hockey club, and ODK Leadership Society, and was just asked to be involved in a brand-new organization on campus called the Lion Ambassadors. My initial instinct was to say "no," but the more I considered the opportunity being presented to me, the more I realized it was the right thing to do. The experience turned out to be mutually beneficial, and I personally grew and matured far more from the relationship than I imagined I would.

Scott Martin was 12 years old when we were introduced and was living with his mother, Peggy, and two sisters, Cheryl and Lori, who really cared about Scott. Scott was a shy and reserved young man and the belief was that he needed a "big brother" in his life. We used our shared passion for hockey to help break the ice (ok, that was pretty corny), and we spent time skating at the rink, going to the movies, studying at the library, and my favorite part, home cooked meals at his mom's house!

Scott and I enjoyed a mutually beneficial and gratifying relationship and the friendship we built helped Scott with school and hockey and me as a mentor. Scott attended school at Williamsport College (Now Penn College) earning an associate degree in Construction Management with an emphasis in Residential and Commercial Construction. He is the proud owner of Scott Martin Homes in Butler, PA, which has been very successful for over 17 years! When I had dinner with Scott and his family in their home (that he built!), Scott was wearing a shirt that said, "Live by the Code: Learn It, Live It, Build It."

Scott married a gem of a woman in Jackie, a 6th grade teacher, and they have two sons, both of whom played hockey. Andrew, a high school junior, and Christopher, who is in his freshman year of college studying aviation and is on an Air Force ROTC Scholarship with an eye on becoming a pilot. Scott is a pilot himself and has been active as a youth hockey coach and board officer for youth hockey and is driven by his passion to help young people.

Scott is now mentoring a young man who wants to learn the construction business from a practitioner. Scott has embraced a philosophy to "pay it forward" and you can hear the joy in his voice of being a mentor himself. Scott tells kids, "You need to develop your own passions. Discover what you love to do. Don't just follow along what others are doing. There is nothing wrong with learning a trade, there is something no-ble in working hard and earning your paycheck doing what you are good at and see it develop into a passion."

Business owner, devoted husband and father, amateur pilot, volunteer, and mentor. Now that's a successful life in my book and I couldn't be prouder of the person that Scott has become.

Your current mentors are:

1. _____

2. _____

3. _____

4. _____

5. _____

People you would like to approach about mentoring:

1. _____

2. _____

3. _____

4. _____

5. _____

Mentorship brought together lifelong friends
Joe Battista and Scott Martin.

2. Everyone Needs a Coach!

"Everyone needs a coach... We all need people who will give us feedback. That's how we improve." **Bill Gates Co-Founder of Microsoft**

A coach is different from a mentor. According to *Management Mentors*, coaching is task-oriented, short term, and performance driven. Mentoring is relationship oriented, long term, and development driven. In many cases you will pay a coach to provide their expertise in assisting you in developing a specific skill. Think along the lines of paying a tutor at school, a personal fitness instructor, or an executive business coach.

We don't seem to hesitate to pay a lot of money to hire a private athletic coach, music teacher, dance teacher, or fitness instructor. You should consider hiring a coach when you have a specific skill that needs to be developed such as improving your study skills, reading speed and comprehension, time management, confidence, college selection, resume writing, financial planning, and career and life planning.

You have probably spent money at some point in your life on camps, clinics, and private instructors for sports, interests, and activities that will likely never directly result in an economic gain for you. So why do we have this stigma about hiring a coach to help us learn about "Life 101," career planning, or running a business?

I have benefited greatly over the years from both volunteer and professional coaches, some who provide their services for free, others as part of their job within an organization, and some that I simply paid as an investment in myself. You need to get past whatever the critics might think and seek out assistance when you need it.

Some of my coaches over the years include:

Dr. Dave Yukelson, Sports Psychologist, "The Coaches Coach," who helped me to learn how to better relate to the athletes I coached and develop personal coping strategies.

Dr. Bob Slaney, Clinical Psychologist, who helped me with anger issues after a serious family issue. **Chris Bahr**, Financial Coach and Representative at Cambridge Investment Research, helped my wife and me to become better at managing our kids' college funds and our retirement and investment funds. **Cindy Cornell**, Principal of The Hoshin Group, and a Leadership and Executive Coach, who helped me to gain the confidence to start my own consulting business. **Tammy Miller**, a Speech and Life Coach, who showed me how to be a better speaker and to learn the professional speaker industry.

Think of specific areas of your personal or professional life where you may need an expert coach to help you overcome an obstacle or develop a skill to advance your career.

"A coach is someone who tells you what you don't want to hear, who has you see what you don't want to see, so you can be who you have always known you could be." **Tom Landry, NFL Hall of Fame Coach**

You may need a coach for:

1. _____

2. _____

3. _____

Coaching session on career exploration with High School graduate Jamie B. and her mother, Wendy, as we discuss her "next steps" in her career exploration.
[*Courtesy of Jon Battista*]

Objective 4: Find your daily motivation to live an inspired life!

"Expect more from each other. Demand more from yourself!"
Penn State Icers Team Theme for 1999-2000

You must discover ways to positively motivate yourself daily through intentional use of music, YouTube videos, podcasts, books, coaching, meditation, and exercise, and have the mindset to develop a willingness to push yourself beyond your current status.

1. Get Up and Take Purposeful, Passionate Action

Wake up inspired! Find a strategy that gets you going especially on those days when you need to just grind it out. Getting a great start to the day is incredibly beneficial. Your chances of getting off to a great start actually begins with preparation the night before. Get all the things you need for the next day readied or at least started so you wake up ready to "come alive" and attack your day with energy and enthusiasm!

As a kid I was fascinated by NASA and the space program and the "Space Race" that bonded the country and gave us hope in our quest to land a man on the moon as inspired by President John F. Kennedy. Anytime there was a countdown on television, it was exhilarating. You heard the famous launch sequence, "5-4-3-2-1 ignition, **and liftoff!**" It got your blood pumping and your heart racing, and you literally felt fired up!

In her new book *The Five Second Rule*, Mel Robbins (contributing editor to *SUCCESS* magazine), has taken the launch countdown and applied it to everyday life. At the moments when you have the need to act (such as waking up in the morning), you simply do your own version of a launch countdown and count backwards "5-4-3-2-1" and you get up and move before your mind stops you from acting. A simple but brilliant strategy!

What you don't want to do is keep hitting the snooze button. Don't just lie in bed wasting time reading social media or answering emails. **Get up and get into the action habit!** While you are in your morning routine, listen to uplifting music or even a short podcast or motivational video. I have a short prayer hanging in my shower that I read intentionally every morning. When I reach the line *"fill me with your spirit"* I take a deep breath as an affirmation to get me "in the flow" spiritually. Once you are dressed, refreshed, and energized, take a minute to review your schedule for the day to verify it. Drink a full glass of water before you drink coffee, tea, or juice, then eat, and read a short blog post or review news headlines (if needed for your job!).

If you are an early riser, this is a good time to get in 20-30 minutes of personal and professional development reading. If not, stay focused and get to classes or work on time.

2. Daily Motivational Tips

"Every morning we are born again. What we do today is what matters most." **Buddha**

As noted previously, start your day off with something positive. Stretch while listening to positive music, drink a tall glass of water, give yourself a positive affirmation ("Today is my day to be awesome!"), or go for a brisk walk or jog. I start every morning immediately with a full glass of water then read a short devotional from my *Coach's Bible* and a short email message from best-selling author and mentor Seth Godin. Then it's a walk with the dog.

What do you do every day to motivate you and help you get through the day?

Throughout the day feed your mind and body by staying hydrated and getting up at least once an hour to walk and get the blood flowing. Also, schedule time in your day to intentionally read a blog post, listen to a podcast, or watch a short motivational video. I switch up sources between subject matter experts like Jack Canfield, Brian Tracy, Jordan Peterson, Mel Robbins, Tony Robbins, Neen James, Gary Vaynerchuk, and my friend Marty Wolff's *The Business Builder's Show*.

Pragmatic Point: You can listen to podcasts during "the waiting times" – waiting in line for coffee, between classes or meetings, or on your drive home.

I also get weekly emails from The Napoleon Hill Foundation, Walk the Talk Motivation, Art Petty, Jim Rohn, and Brian Tracy among others. Finally, because there just aren't enough hours in the day, I have a subscription to Soundview Executive Book Summaries. It allows me to read or listen to excerpts and summaries from the newest literary offerings before deciding to purchase the book.

These aren't the only ways to motivate you, though. The power of music can motivate you too, so be intentional in selecting your songs. Certain music puts you in different moods. Find the right mix of songs for you. I am big on instrumental music in the category of "relaxed but energized," especially inspiring movie soundtracks. One of the best I have found recently is *Epic Instrumental* by Fearless Motivation.

My Songs for Motivation: "Thunder" – Imagine Dragons, "I Can See Clearly Now" – Johnny Nash, "Heart of A Champion" – Nelly, "The Best Day of My Life" – American Authors, "Feeling Stronger Everyday" – Chicago, "On the Loose" – Saga, "If Today Was Your Last Day" – Nickelback

Movie Soundtracks for Inspiration: *The Dark Knight Rises, The Rock, The Greatest Showman, Rudy, Creed, Hoosiers, Rocky;* Anything from Hans Zimmer and James Horner.

Powerful Playlists: My playlists are broken into the following categories: Inspiration, Work, Introspection, Mellow, Workout 1, and Workout 2.

1. What songs with a positive message do you listen to most often?

2. What apps do you have on your smartphone for podcasts, webcasts, etc.?

3. What blogs do you read for personal or professional development?

4. What routine do you have to develop your spirit and practice mindfulness? (See Chapter 3, Objective 1 on mindfulness.)

"Music is one of the most powerful neurobiological tools we have to change our mood, mindset, and behavior." **Christopher Bergland, World-Class Endurance Athlete, Coach, and Author**

3. Be Mentally Tough

You cannot control every negative person or circumstance that comes your way. But you can apply the attitude principles from Chapter 2 and choose to deflect, ignore, or cope with any perceived micro-aggressions or circumstances beyond your control. There are certain battles worth fighting and others where you are better off having thick skin and letting hurtful comments simply roll off your back. Don't give the hater trying to rattle you the satisfaction! Sometimes the best defense is a simple smile and to walk away, so they're left wondering what you know that they don't!

Remember the parent, teacher, coach, or boss who gave you an emotionally charged butt chewing or even used sarcasm to make a point? They may really just be trying to motivate you, either purposely or serendipitously. There is something to be learned from every experience, good or bad. Sometimes it is best to not listen to *how* someone says something to you, but rather *what* they say. Filtering through the negatives can still yield good advice or ideas. It's what you make of it that matters.

We cannot go back and undo the past, but we can learn from it. We can try to make amends for any perceived transgressions, we can ask for forgiveness, and we can give forgiveness. I wish I could go back in time to do the right thing and stand up for that seemingly awkward kid from junior high who was being bullied (you know, the one that went on to become a successful doctor). Instead, I can teach today's kids to be more respectful, so they can be stronger at another moment of truth.

Give yourself permission to move forward and cut loose any baggage that might be holding you back. Regardless of the obstacles and adversity you face, you will get over it faster if you have a mentally tough mindset and get back to focusing on your purpose as soon as you can.

"Life always gives you a second chance. It's called TOMOR-ROW." **Anonymous**

I have an entire file drawer full of motivational sayings and have several quotes and sayings framed that hang on the walls in my home. Hey, I was a coach after all! One that I have had since college is a picture hanging in my home office of Nadia Comaneci, five-time Olympic gold medalist, doing an incredibly difficult maneuver on the balance beam. It has been an inspiration for me and for anyone who has ever been in my office. It says:

"Do not pray for an easy life. Pray to be a strong person."

List your favorite positive inspirational sayings:

_____

_____

_____

_____

_____

Do not pray
for an easy life.
Pray to be a strong person.

Keep your favorite quotes and inspirational
photos where you can see them daily.

Chapter 5 Summary:

1. Find your inspiration.

2. Surround yourself with great people who will challenge you to be better.

3. Find your mentors and coaches.

4. Find your daily motivation to live an inspired life!

I hope you found this to be a fun chapter that can help you find the inspiration and motivation to achieve your personal and professional goals. **Get with your Pragmatic Passion Partner and go over the questions below:**

1. Where do you intentionally seek inspiration?

_____

_____

_____

2. Who have you identified that you know must be removed from your life, or at least minimize contact with, who has been a negative influence or enabler of bad habits?

_____

_____

_____

3. Who are the people you want to be in your life more often, who believe in you, and will be supportive, but honest with you when necessary?

_____

_____

_____

4. Write down exactly what you would like a mentor or coach to work on with you.

_____

_____

_____

5. Do you need a professional coach in your life? If money is an issue, can you identify someone who might be willing to assist as a volunteer?

_____

_____

_____

6. Write down a week's worth of daily motivational songs and sayings that will inspire you every morning and at other times when you need it.

_____

_____

_____

"Success isn't what others can see, but how you feel. It's living your truth and doing what makes you truly happy. That's Success." **Robert Tew, www.livelifehappy.com**

Chapter 6
Options

"Dreams without goals are just dreams, and that ultimately leads to disappointment."

Denzel Washington, Academy Award Winner and Professional Speaker

Chapter 6 Objectives:

1. The decision-making process

2. How to set goals that are based in reality

3. Educational and career decisions that make sense

We are a result of our choices. We must own our choices, the judgments we make, and be held accountable for our actions.

Every decision we make has consequences, whether good or bad, intended or unintended. How you make decisions - the deliberate process you consistently follow - is critical to achieving personal and professional success. Learning how to develop better options and to make more informed choices is a skill you will continue to develop throughout your life. Give this skill the intentional and deliberate time and practice it requires.

We all know people who suffer from excusitis and like to throw themselves pity parties. Some people believe personal and professional success is based on luck and fate alone. No doubt that some degree of success can be attributed to serendipity, the luck of the draw, or being in the right place at the right time.

I choose to believe in my heart that "luck favors the prepared." Through education and experience gained from work, exploring, and trying new things, we put ourselves in a position to be "lucky."

"Failure is not an option!" Those were the words spoken by Gene Kranz, flight director of *Apollo 13*, after an explosion crippled the spacecraft and NASA engineers had to figure out options for bringing the three astronauts home safely.

If you want to see a good example of the application of "developing options and making informed choices," spend a few minutes watching the iconic scene from the 1995 movie *Apollo 13*, when the NASA engineers had to find a timely solution under tremendous stress to bring back the capsule that was running out of power, oxygen, and communications.

Objective 1: The Decision-Making Process

"We are prone to blame decision makers for good decisions that worked out badly and to give them too little credit for successful moves that appear obvious only after the fact." **Daniel Kahneman, Thinking, Fast and Slow**

Envision a carpenter preparing to cut a piece of wood. Pressed for time, he takes clumsy measurements and quickly saws through the wood—but the final product is uneven, splintered, and unusable for the rest of the project. In this scenario, the popular proverb rings true: "Measure twice, cut once." It is often better to spend intentional time thinking through a decision to ensure the best course of action than to make an impulsive choice hastily and suffer the consequences.

The best times to make these precise "measurements" are at stages of your life that may dictate the future of your education or career. These junctures can be big or small—as significant as deciding whether to accept a job offer, or as simple as Googling the basics about a college to see whether you are interested in applying. The key is to practice patient, purposeful thinking, develop a Plan A and a Plan B, and be prepared with whatever else you need before implementation. Be conscious of the weight that critical decisions bear—just like the carpenter with the unusable, splintered piece of wood, once you make a life-altering decision it is often everlasting and difficult to reverse.

There are many times when a good decision made in a timely manner is better than the perfect solution implemented too late. This is especially true with less important decisions like deciding what restaurant to try for dinner. It might be an urgent decision, but if you spend all day deciding, you may not get reservations in time. For more critical decisions that require more research and discussion, such as whether to pursue higher education or learn a trade or switch jobs mid-career, it is more useful to utilize the problem-solving techniques that will be discussed in the following pages.

It is also true that all too often people make their decisions based solely on emotion. While I am considered an "inspirational speaker," it is often frustrating when I see people get all fired up after hearing a single motivational talk and believe immediately afterward they can become an expert in a given discipline or industry. I believe that you go to hear professional speakers to be inspired or motivated when you need a spark to start or the proverbial "kick in the butt" to be reminded to stick to your plan.

To change behaviors and make real progress toward your goals, you need more than a pump-up speech to make pragmatic decisions. You need a burning desire to learn, and you need a coach or an accountability partner who will keep you on track. It isn't very pragmatic, for instance, to believe you can listen to one speech and suddenly go off to the bank tomorrow to borrow money and become a Dunkin' Donuts or McDonald's franchisee. Without really knowing what it means to own and operate a franchise, you are likely to become just another small business bankruptcy statistic. Do your due diligence and research the upside and downside of your important decisions.

Yes, friends, family, media "experts," and professionals will want to give you their two cents. But, at the end of the day, it is up to you to process that information and move forward with a choice and act to "Get It Done." This personal responsibility and accountability requires courage.

Listen, whether big or small, a slew of decisions need to be made every day. Sometimes these decisions will overwhelm you. Sometimes your best choice is not always clear. And sometimes you'll have trouble knowing where to turn for help if a complicated situation arises. When this happens, take a deep breath and use the tools in this chapter to figure out how to make the best and most informed decisions you can to ensure that each of your days is purposeful and contributing to a successful future!

1. Applying The 7 Principles: Ask Better Questions to Help Make Better Decisions

Whenever you have a tough decision to make, consider applying one or all of the 7 Pragmatic Passion Principles to help put your options into perspective. Ask yourself the following questions with regard to your most important choices:

1. Does it support my values, passions, and **purpose**?

2. Will I have the proper **attitude** to commit to and act on my purpose?

3. Am I willing to make the **sacrifices** to persist and persevere along the way?

4. Does the decision serve others first and align with my **servant leadership** philosophy?

5. Will I be **inspired** to pursue my purpose with passion to "Get It Done?"

6. Will I devote the time to develop the best **options** so I make informed choices?

7. Will it **nurture** me so I may live a joyful, fulfilling, passionate, and purposeful life?

Best-selling author Suzy Welch has several YouTube videos where she discusses what she calls the "10-10-10 Rule." To help put into perspective how decisions you make now can have a ripple effect into the future, she advises that you ask yourself:

1. How will I feel about this 10 minutes from now?

2. What about 10 months from now?

3. What about 10 years from now?

Essentially what I take from this is to practice "situational awareness" and to do "scenario planning" PRIOR to taking decisive action. This prevents irrational and impulsive reactions to help you make more informed decisions.

1. **Situational Awareness:** Gather all the pertinent, timely information that is available. Be aware of the current internal and external factors before making decisions. Be

aware of timing, context, perceptions, and your environment.

2. **Scenario Planning:** Develop options by creating scenarios and assessing potential outcomes. Use poise and patience to vet out potential decisions so you might discover and even predict unintended consequences. Avoid making the cure worse than the ailment.

"Keep everything in proper perspective. You don't need to pole vault over mouse turds." **Dick Bartolomea**

2. The Eisenhower-Covey Decision Matrix

There are many decision-making models and I encourage you to explore several until you find the one that works for you. A time-tested model that I have used throughout my career is known as the Eisenhower-Covey Decision Matrix, named after former President Dwight D. Eisenhower and expanded upon by Dr. Stephen Covey.

The model is centered on distinguishing what is "urgent" and what is "important." Urgent tasks are those that must be dealt with immediately and usually put us in a defensive "reactive mode" due to its pressing nature. Important tasks are vital as well, but do not have the same dire connotations. Instead, important tasks contribute to long-term goals. Unlike Urgent Mode, in the Important Mode we do not panic or revert to survival instincts; instead, we operate calmly and with purpose.

In his bestselling book *The 7 Habits of Highly Effective People*, Dr. Stephen Covey took Eisenhower's core principles and created the Eisenhower-Covey Decision Matrix. The matrix is divided into four quadrants:

- **Important and Urgent**

- **Important** but not urgent

- **Urgent** but not important

- Not important not urgent

You can use this model to organize the tasks in your life into one of these four quadrants and determine if your time is being utilized wisely. The model is a wonderful tool to help you navigate the path of life, which is often rocky and lacks the proper directional signage.

NOTE: For a more in-depth look at using the Eisenhower-Covey Decision Matrix go to **www.PragmaticPassion.com/ bookresources**

Another simple way of organizing your work is by putting tasks into three categories:

1. Can you do it yourself?

2. Does it require the help of others or would it be better to give to someone else?

3. Is it required or necessary? If it's not worth your time and attention, and not a task assigned by a superior, then perhaps the best choice is to dump it. For example, junk mail and emails.

Pragmatic Point: Decision-making is a blending of: art and science, of data analysis and intuition, of decisiveness and poise, of pragmatism and passion. **Prepare - Validate - Do!**

"Prepare-Validate-Do" is equivalent to "Ready, aim, fire!" With all due respect to Nike's "Just Do It" slogan, you need to prepare and plan before just doing! Avoid the emotionally driven "Fire, ready, aim!" or the bureaucratic "Ready, ready, ready... Should we aim? Let's table it and give it to a committee." Choose the "Prepare-Validate-Do!" method to get things done!

3. Analytics or Intuition? You need both!

"The most dangerous phrase in the language is, 'We've always done it this way.'" **U.S. Navy Rear Admiral Grace Hopper, Computer Pioneer and First Woman to Earn a Ph.D. in Mathematics from Yale University (1939)**

Rear Admiral Grace Hopper, known affectionately to her colleagues as "Amazing Grace," was a trailblazer and "disruptor" of her era from 1945-1986. She challenged conventional wisdom and broke down gender barriers while advancing the role of computers to new levels.

I imagine that when a colleague would put down one of her new ideas with the standard, "We've always done it this way around here," Grace's response would be something like, "Well, *currently* we do it this way. I bet you have an idea for how we might improve the process, right?" Sometimes asking a disarming question gets your antagonist to think outside the box. Suddenly, they are more open to your idea, because they think it was their idea!

Just as passion is a necessary, but not sufficient, ingredient for determining your career path, so it is with data analytics and intuition. This is especially true when making complicated business and research decisions. Alone, each is necessary but not sufficient in making the best decisions. Having a lot of data is great, but unless it can be interpreted, and conclusions can be drawn that lead to consistently good decisions, it could be just useless information. Likewise, intuition alone that ignores obvious data based facts, will usually lead to poor outcomes. Analytics and intuition are tools in your toolbox that have a synergistic benefit used in harmony.

Pragmatic Point: If you were struggling with a certain problem (say alcoholism), would you want help from a pure researcher or someone who has been through the same battles and beaten it? The answer is...BOTH!

A Pragmatic Analysis is where common sense, empathy, research, proper planning, practice, and repetition intersect to help you arrive at the best choice.

In his June 16, 2014 Dataversity article "Why the Analytics vs. Intuition Debate Misses the Mark," Gil Allouche spells out the synergistic benefits for using both analytics and intuition in decision making:

> The intuition vs. analytics debate, however, is really missing the mark. It's not like businesses only have one choice

between intuition and analytics. It's not an either or situation. Ideally, businesses can use analytics and intuition together to dramatically increase the positive outcomes that come from the decision making process. They'll be able to utilize the best characteristics of both components.

There is a distinct difference between thoroughly thinking through a decision, and waiting too long to take action to implement your plans. Perfect is the enemy of done! If you wait too long for any number of reasons—holding out for more data, or qualitative information, another offer, or some spark of inspiration—the right opportunity may, and often will, pass you by.

There is a quasi-medical name for this particular set of symptoms: "Paralysis by Analysis." According to behavior specialist Manny Rodriguez, Analysis Paralysis is the "state of overthinking a situation so that a decision or action is never taken, in effect paralyzing the outcome." To avoid Analysis Paralysis, Rodriguez suggests to:

- Identify your objectives and your end goal to save time and confusion.

- Give yourself a time limit or a deadline to make the decision.

- Do not "psych" yourself out by thinking of your past Analysis Paralysis situations. The brain is a powerful thing—if you tell yourself you are bad at decision-making, history is bound to repeat itself!

You must embrace a strategy that uses the best of both worlds by doing the appropriate research and using your own instincts and critical thinking skills to arrive at pragmatic and timely conclusions.

Objective 2: Setting Pragmatic Goals That Are Based In Reality

Graduation and Commencement speakers around the country typically have a few pearls of wisdom that sound remarkably the same everywhere you go. "Follow your dreams," "Find your passions," "Shoot for the moon, even if you miss you will land among the stars," "Do what you love," "Listen to your heart," and of course…"Just go for it!" They have become so overused that Katie Palmer designed a BINGO card in a humorous article for *Wired* entitled, "Graduations Are Way Less Awful with Commencement Bingo."

If all this advice were really true and as simple to implement as it sounds, perhaps we would not have a national mental health crisis going on, record levels of adult children living with their parents, 70% of our workers disengaged at their jobs, and a middle class on the verge of financial ruin.

In a 2018 study from Stanford Psychologist Dr. Carol Dweck (author of **Mindset, the New Psychology of Success**) and Yale researcher Dr. Paul O'Keefe, they warn that the common advice to simply "find your passion" is actually bad advice. O'Keefe says that developing a passion is better advice because it is an active process that depends more on your efforts to explore and grow as a person. Dweck believes that possessing a "growth mindset" will help you determine your true interests and passions and therefore have the willpower to master them.

I love to hear commencement speakers who tell you the truth. Life is hard. It is a grind. It is full of unforeseen challenges and obstacles. Setbacks are unavoidable and there will be times of pain. But, they will also tell you that life is full of wonderful and amazing moments, exhilarating experiences, laughter, and tears of joy. There is a feeling so deeply rewarding from putting in a hard day's work and in rising from a fall.

Delivering the commencement speech titled "Confidence, Courage, and Persistence" to the Smeal College of Business Executive MBA Class of 2017.
[*Photo Courtesy of Stephanie Errigo*]

If you plan wisely, if you put time into well thought out strategies based on the best current information, if you seek out help from your team of advisors, if you put in the necessary time to learn new skills - you will develop the confidence and the courage to take on almost anything that comes your way. Now that is a commencement speech worth hearing!

1. The Pragmatic Passion Graph – An Intuitive Illustration

Look at the Pragmatic Passion Graph on page 219. Where do you currently see yourself on the Passion axis (the vertical line)? Are you "Low Passion" at the bottom of the vertical axis, "High Passion" at the top, or at some point between?

Where are you currently on the Pragmatic axis? Are you "Low Pragmatism" at the far left of the horizontal axis, "High Pragmatism" at the far right, or at some point between? Look in the mirror and be honest.

After you plot yourself along each axis, where is your current "Pragmatic Passion Intersection" on the graph?

Are you The Fantasizer, The Dud, The Minimalist, or The Real Deal? Be honest with yourself. I am sure you know people who fit into each of the four quadrants and one of the nine categories below. The goal, of course, is to reach the high passion, high pragmatism quadrant and be as close to The Real Deal as possible. It's where you are living a fulfilling, authentic, and purposeful life, as well as being a high performer and team player.

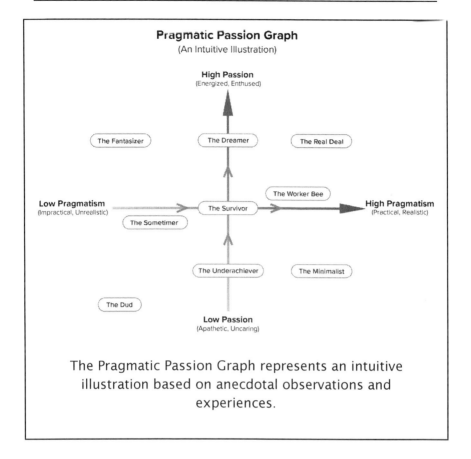

The Pragmatic Passion Graph represents an intuitive illustration based on anecdotal observations and experiences.

For the purposes of this exercise use the following definitions:

"The Real Deal" (High Passion, High Pragmatism)

- Fulfilled

- Purposeful

- High Performer

"The Dreamer" (High Passion, Medium Pragmatism)

- Good Ideas

- Inconsistent

- Big Talker

"The Fantasizer" (High Passion, Low Pragmatism)

- Idealistic

- Utopian

- No Action

"The Sometimer" (Medium Passion, Low Pragmatism)

- Average Worker

- Minimal Skills

- Undependable

"The Survivor" (Medium Passion, Medium Pragmatism)

- Just Gets By

- Just There

- Fence-sitter

"The Worker Bee" (Medium Passion, High Pragmatism)

- Productive

- Efficient

- Dependable

"The Minimalist" (Low Passion, High Pragmatism)

- Gets Job Done

- Unsatisfied

- Unfulfilled

"The Underachiever" (Low Passion, Medium Pragmatism)

- Has Skills

- Disinterested

- Needs Constant Supervision

"The Dud" (Low Passion, Low Pragmatism)

- Uninspired

- Unmotivated

- Unreliable

While further research for the graph is still in the works, common sense allows for this anecdotal "illustration" of where you might currently see yourself. **More importantly, where do you see yourself in the future?**

2. Five Tips for Successful Goal Setting:

Here are five strategies I have learned over the years for successful goal setting:

1. You must put your goals in writing and you must post them where you will see them every day.

2. Set a realistic and attainable main objective that aligns with your purpose. Then, set short-term goals that will lead to achieving your bigger, medium-range and long-term goals.

3. Put together a plan of action with milestones to manage your progress. Set pragmatic deadlines that allow for the time to properly achieve your objectives.

4. Do periodic evaluations of your progress (working with Your Pragmatic Passion Partner or a coach) and make necessary adjustments as needed.

5. Take time to modestly and safely celebrate achieving milestones, especially with those who helped you!

Make goal setting an intentional and purposeful daily practice and the results will prove themselves out over time.

"A goal is a dream with a deadline! Get into the ACTION habit!" **Dr. David Schwartz, Author of The Magic of Getting What You Want**

3. Positive Fantasizing Or Pragmatic Passion?

"When the world becomes a fantasy, and you're more than you could ever be, 'cause you're dreaming with your eyes wide open." **"Come Alive" from the Greatest Showman**

A friend posted a great meme on Facebook that said, "May your life one day be as fabulous as you pretend it is on Facebook." You don't typically see people posting about their failures on social media, do you? We are drawn to the stories where dreams come true and people appear to live these perfect lives. We tend to downplay or even avoid the stories that don't turn out so well. The difference between a dream based in fantasy, and one based in reality, is the essence of Pragmatic Passion.

Remember the research by Dr. Gabriele Oettingen discussed in the introduction? While I do believe that positive thinking is a necessary ingredient for success, it is, like passion, not enough. According to Dr. Oettingen and many of her colleagues, it may actually hurt your chances of succeeding if you do not put in the required time, discipline, and action necessary to achieve your biggest, boldest dreams.

Many of us dream of "making it big" as a CEO of a global company or as a multi-millionaire entrepreneur, or a world-famous celebrity. We know it can be done. But, don't fool yourself into thinking it's going to be easy. It takes an extreme effort to successfully climb the corporate ladder, to start a business from scratch and to scale it, and to "make it" in Hollywood, on Broadway, or as a professional athlete.

Passion Point: If you are deeply passionate about pursuing your interests in one of these highly competitive fields, and you are willing to commit to it with your heart and soul, then you must have the mindset that you will succeed and the mental toughness to persevere.

In reality, there are relatively few business executives, entrepreneurs, celebrities, entertainers, and professional athletes with all the skills and talents necessary to reach the top in these highly competitive fields.

There are even fewer celebrities (the starving artist) and pro athletes (considering the vast majority toil in the minor leagues) who actually make enough money to live the lavish lifestyles we tend to see on social media and television, that would last them throughout their lives.

Their talents, hard work, and perhaps good fortune have provided them a life of fame and seemingly endless prosperity. They are considered role models to other aspiring artists, musicians, and athletes across the nation. In reality, those with staying power got there with incredible sacrifices, hard work, perseverance, and yes, some breaks along the way.

If you believe yourself to be in this elite category, then gear up, roll up your sleeves, and get at it! But, go into it with your eyes wide-open as to the sacrifices it will take. As we know, passion alone is not enough. Let me add that hope is not a reliable strategy, either. This is where a Pragmatic Passion mindset can assist in helping you to make the hard choices about where to invest your time, money, and efforts.

For example, here are some hard facts about the difficulty in "making it big" as an actor or singer:

According to NPR, of the 49,000 members of Actors' Equity Association, the professional theatre actors union, only around 17,000 members are estimated to actually work in any year.

Of the members who do work, the median income from work in theatre is approximately $7,500 a year. That's $144/week. The average unemployment rate for actors, according to the Actors' Equity Association, hovers around 90 percent.

Many actors leave the business after a few years. Many musicians and singers find only part-time or intermittent work and may have long periods of unemployment between jobs.

The stress of constantly looking for work leads many to accept permanent full-time jobs in other occupations while working part time as a musician or singer. For the vast majority, this is the lifestyle. As long as you understand this, it could allow you to have the best of all worlds.

Here are some hard facts about the difficulty in "making it big" in athletics:

- Of all high school athletes, only 6% will make a team roster in any of the 3 NCAA Divisions (I, II, or II) and only 1.9% will compete at the NCAA Division 1 Level.

- The odds of college athletes ever playing in professional leagues are even tougher: WNBA: 1%, NBA: 1.1%, NFL: 1.5%, MLS: 1.4%.

- Of the 480,000 NCAA athletes, only 2% will ever make it to the pros and the average length of a pro career is 3.4 years, even for those who do beat the odds.

For more of a glimpse at the odds of "making it big" in sports or entertainment go to **www.PragmaticPassion.com/ bookresources**.

I am a strong proponent of playing competitive sports and getting involved in a variety of extracurricular activities if, and only if, people take a pragmatic view of the landscape and have more realistic expectations of the outcomes. It's why they should remember the positive developmental benefits first and foremost and understand the very difficult odds of actually earning a scholarship and going on to make a livable wage professionally.

"We believe Student-Athletes have hidden competencies (skills and knowledge) they don't even know they have that are highly valuable in business." **Brad Mitchell, Founder and CEO, National Athletic and Professional Success Academy**

Unfortunately, I fear far too many parents are living vicariously through their kids, throwing more and more money at trainers, clinics, academies, private lessons, travel sports, and showcases.

I have absolutely no problem with investing a certain amount of time and money on additional training, but more and more research is showing the negative impact of overtraining at early ages due to this obsession with sports success. The rise in "repetitive use" injuries such as tennis elbow, stress fractures, and concussions is just the physical toll we see.

Important time and attention are also lost for academic development if you are in the wrong program that has the wrong priorities. It's especially disconcerting when the experiences turn out negative from out of control and abusive coaches and instructors seeking only to increase their reputations for their own financial gain.

There are certainly kids who are naturally gifted in athletics, music, and art and it makes sense for them to consider special training at a certain point in their progression because they have the raw talent that gives them a solid base. You may be, or have been, or you have kids that might be one of them, and if so, great! If you have a few unbiased sources that have validated that you have exceptional talent, then by all means go for it.

Pursuing private training may only be worthwhile if you also have the desire, instincts, and aptitude necessary to be successful. Validate this before investing your time, energy, and money.

"I've seen parents spend a couple of hundred thousand dollars pursuing a college scholarship. They could have set it aside to pay for the damn college." **Travis Dorsch, Director of the Families in Sport Lab at Utah State University**

My advice to anyone or any parent is always to use a pragmatic, common sense approach.

Don't put all your hopes in the athletic scholarship basket, because the odds are still heavily against the vast majority of student-athletes. Seek out programs where part of the development includes an emphasis on academics, including time management, study skills, coping skills and goal setting.

In essence, developing skills so you have a plan B for your future. Proper sportsmanship and behavior should also be a part of the right curriculum.

Sports organizations that are run properly know this. They aren't trying to sell you a bill of goods and false hopes. Sports done right, like most extracurricular activities, can develop positive character traits and good life skills. As always, apply your Pragmatic Passion Philosophy before making a commitment.

My challenge to you is to go back to your passion, your purpose, and your vision statement and let that guide your decision-making process. Whether you are a teenager (or their parent) deciding on post-secondary plans; a young adult trying to pivot and find a direction, an adult going through a career transition, or a retiree looking to make an impact as a volunteer or to start a new venture, you must do your research and take the common-sense approach to making informed decisions.

The time we spend on our interests and hobbies (avocations) such as practicing the violin, taking singing or dance lessons, or getting up for a 5:00 am swimming or skating practice are not wasted if done in a pragmatic way with reasonable expectations and outcomes. Learning the benefits of dedication, teamwork, time management, perseverance, patience, staying physically fit, and developing social skills are usually well worth the time and effort.

Pragmatic Point: If you cannot make enough money to meet your desired quality of life, by focusing only on doing something you love to do, **then you must be prepared to pivot.**

4. A Vocation that Provides for an Avocation.

There are many examples of people who work at a job that pays the bills, provides benefits, and offers security, while allowing them the time and flexibility to fulfill their passions as an avocation or hobby.

I am passionate about golf. I would play every day if possible. You may be equally passionate about playing music in a band, riding horses, playing video games online, or playing poker with great friends. But the clear majority of us are not good enough at our hobbies to be paid to play. We continue to invest time and money on these passions because of the joy they bring.

You may have a similar love of an activity that you always dreamed could lead to a paid career but have come to a realization that it just isn't going to happen. Well, here is the good news. You can find a job and career that can pay you enough money to live a quality of life that will make you happy, allow you the time and resources to pursue some of your passions as avocations or hobbies, and allow you to move toward your purpose. With purposeful planning, that is possible.

And while we should certainly strive to find that career that allows us to get paid for something we are deeply passionate about, not everyone can get paid for what they love to do...at least not in the short run.

So, it's imperative that you find a career path doing something you are good at where you can take a great attitude to work every day. Perhaps you can find the job that allows you the flexibility to volunteer in an activity or organization that fulfills your purpose. Then, the job becomes a means to an end, so you can fulfill your purpose.

Real Life 101: A Career and a Passion That Align with a Purpose

Laura Ann Saxe has been passionate about theatre and entertainment since she was a young girl growing up in a music-loving household in Chicago. She dreamed of being on stage and performing in a theatrical group. Her voice and music lessons earned her the opportunity to perform with the Chicagoland Theatrical Troupe in high school. She found incredible joy in performing. Alas, an injury, which required surgery, temporarily put her dreams on hold.

After being operated on by Dr. Theodore Fox, the Chicago Bears team orthopedic doctor, she developed a passion to be a nurse. It was her fascination with the work done by his staff nurse Joanie that piqued Laura Ann's interest and touched her heart. Laura Ann discovered that her purpose was to serve others, one way or another. Realizing that the life of a theatre performer was hard and transient, she decided to attend college to study nursing. But she stayed involved in theatre and auditioned and was selected for the cast at the Marriott's Great American Theme Park where she worked for three summers. She met her future husband Dave, a school-teacher, through their shared passion for the theatre. They thought about making the theatre a career and decided to go for it and auditioned for various roles. Laura Ann's first pro-fessional Actors' Equity job was in *Music Man,* and she con-tinued to land industry work for over three years (including starring in a one-year run of *Annie*) and even danced for a television special for ABC.

Soon they learned the harsh realities of life as professional performers, as they witnessed very few of their peers work-ing in stable roles and they led very difficult lives. So Dave went back to school to get his master's and Ph.D. and Laura Ann went to work as a full-time nurse. Eventually Professor Saxe earned a faculty position at two well-known universi-ties. But the couple's passion for the local theatre never waned.

The couple now own and operate a summer theatre, the Nittany Theatre at the Barn. They saved this iconic theatre that has been recognized by the U.S. Congress as one of the oldest operating Barn Theatres in the country. So while Laura Ann's "real" job is as a nurse in a private practice and Dave's is as a college professor of history, it's these jobs, which they both enjoy, that pay their bills. This in turn allows them the opportunity to pursue their passion for acting and entertaining others. Laura Ann and Dave are servant leaders by definition as they find tremendous joy and purpose in serving, healing, teaching, entertaining, and helping others to live better lives.

Objective 3: Educational and Career Decisions That Make Sense

"Two roads diverged in a wood and I - I took the one less traveled by, and that has made all the difference." **Robert Frost, Pulitzer Prize Winning Poet**

People are always in search of the answer to the age-old question, "Do you know what you want to be when you grow up?" as if this is a finite, one-and-done activity. The landscape has changed and there are more opportunities to develop the skills you need to be prepared for work in the 21st century. More and more non-traditional and non-linear approaches to education and career paths are now available.

So, let's turn the clock back again to my experiences. Did I make good choices in high school? What would I do differently if I knew then what I know now? What advice would I give the 18-year-old version of myself? In reality, I was not even close to being ready to go to college after high school. I had no idea what I valued, nor did I even think about what living a purposeful life in service of others meant.

So why did I go to college at 18? Because that is what society tells us to do, whether we are ready or not. I was just another one of the sheep being led wherever society said I should go. Neither of my parents were able to afford college, so while they were supportive (especially helping with my college finances), neither was able to give me that experiential guidance. With the cost of college so high, it is no longer pragmatic to simply go to school to try and figure things out once you get there.

I switched majors four times in my first two years in college and ultimately ended up in the College of Business where I should have been all along. My Division of Undergraduate Studies counselor, Jim Kelly, had me take those personality and interest assessments we talked about in Chapter 1. Based on the results, and with the professional guidance of Mr. Kelly, my life changed forever, for the better.

I have been blessed to live a very fulfilling life with a terrific wife and family and I have very few regrets. Much of what has happened in my life has certainly been the result of hard work, building a strong network, taking advantage of my educational and athletic opportunities, and my faith. I have been the recipient of my share of good fortune and being in the right place at the right time. I could be the poster child for the saying, "Luck is where preparation meets opportunity."

1. Lessons Learned: Make Your Own Path

So, what were the lessons learned? Develop options and make informed choices. First, I would have spent the time and money to have the assessments and subsequent discussion of the results with a professional, while I was in high school. As noted in Chapter 1, we just did this with our youngest son, utilizing the expertise of Bartell and Bartell in State College, PA. It helped him to narrow down his areas of interest dramatically, give deliberate and intentional thought to things that currently matter to him, and to consider what should matter in the future based on his quality of life aspirations.

The naysayers will say: "What 16- or 17-year-old really knows what they want to do?" My response is typically, "You may be right. So why at 18 do we simply ship them off to college? Did they suddenly have an epiphany and become enlightened?" If we start having these discussions in high school, perhaps it will inspire the student to take school more seriously and possibly make more mature decisions (perhaps in their social lives as well).

You are more likely to spend your time effectively in a post-secondary world if you learn how to ask the deep probing questions about what is really important to you. I challenge you to go out and use the science available to at least provide a starting place and to narrow your options, or if you are the parent, for your student. We know that passions and purpose may change depending on your stage of life, but if you are willing to use this strategy, you have a greater chance to set yourself up for success.

Should you go directly to college as an 18-year-old, especially if you consider yourself to be emotionally immature and very uncertain about a major? What other options are available to explore? Should you consider a "gap year" (or two) to work part-time and attend school part-time until you have a better feel for an area of interest? Back when I was in college, college was much more affordable and if you weren't sure "what you wanted to be when you grew up," you essentially used college as a time to search for your passion and purpose.

Today, not so much. We know that according to Bloomberg, college tuition and fees have increased 1,120 percent since 1978 - coincidentally, my freshman year. You read that correctly, 1,120 percent. The purists will insist that colleges are not here to get Jennifer or Johnny a job, only to "broaden their horizons." Sorry, I am calling bull on that one, especially given the out of control costs of a college degree. Colleges are businesses, period. Don't let other people decide your Pragmatic Passion plans. With almost half of those who start college never finishing their degree, why follow the conventional wisdom and end up swamped with debt?

This could be a good time for some self-reflection and a chance to take stock of where you are in your own life's journey, whether you are a student, a parent, a returning adult learner, or a retiree thinking of embarking on a second career. It doesn't matter if you are in high school or college or in a career transition; you have to factor in your definition of success to be able to devise a plan that works for you.

Pragmatic Point: Remember that having a purpose and a passion will lead to a higher probability of a happy and fulfilling career and life.

This is a highly personal and private decision that will affect the rest of your life. Don't go somewhere because of conventional wisdom. You should seek advice and should benchmark, but ultimately you must figure out what is best for you, your personality, and your values. You must also determine what you can really afford and what makes sense in the long haul. The earlier you start, the more information you can gather and the more time you will have to make an informed decision. It is imperative that you develop options and make informed decisions.

If you're a parent of a high-school-age child, then you need to have a serious conversation with your child and you both need to be honest. Unless you both have given this the time and attention it really deserves, and your child has an idea of what they want to be when they grow up, you may want to consider hitting the pause button. Maybe your child isn't ready to go to a four-year school. Even if your child has been recruited or offered an academic or athletic scholarship, if you know they are not emotionally ready or haven't matured enough yet, reconsider sending them to college. They can always request a deferment. Or, maybe they can start in the summer session to get a head start on adjusting to college. It may be that they can wait to enroll in the spring semester if they are not quite ready. Again, we need to look at all options and make the best decision possible. There's no shame in not going directly into college. In fact, if it's the right decision for your child, then it's the smart, responsible choice to make.

Let me ask you this: do you just want to blindly follow the conventional wisdom and risk being another statistic in the college debt mess? Or are you willing to think outside the box and find a plan that makes sense for you and your budget? There are students who work full-time and go to college part-time, and those who work part-time while going to college full-time while incurring little to no debt. Do what makes sense for YOU and not because the marketing pitches of colleges persuade you to do something other than what is pragmatic in your life.

I also believe that being an adult learner is sometimes much better than spending the money right out of high school, especially when you have no idea what direction you want to go. People who have already experienced the real world, perhaps they served in the military, or held several part-time jobs, or possibly failed at another career, tend to appreciate and take better advantage of college.

I see and hear more and more stories of young people and parents mishandling this very important aspect of life and I find myself just shaking my head in frustration. People have no problem spending thousands of dollars on dance lessons and travel sports teams, but won't spend the money or the time to help themselves or loved ones to navigate the waters to find their passion or purpose, and to make informed decisions about their futures.

I am reminded of a rather simple observation from Joseph Murphy's *The Miracle Power of Your Mind*, that states: "Common sense is the most uncommon sense."

How do you make better choices? **By developing pragmatic options and making informed choices.** Here is an example:

Let's say you are passionate about nature and love the outdoors. You enjoy hiking, fishing, camping, traveling to the world's best parks, and you want to live a relatively stress-free life. So, you think, how about working for the National Park Service? But wait. You also want to live in a really nice home, drive a nice 4-wheel drive full-size SUV, aspire to be married and have kids, and want to be able to have vacation time to travel.

So, you check out what it takes to become Park Ranger and consider going to college and getting a degree in biology, forestry, or environmental science. You look at colleges that will cost $40,000 a year "all in" and thankfully your parents will pay half of your tuition, room and board.

Then your Pragmatic Passion, make-informed-decision mindset kicks in and you discover a harsh reality:

According to the U.S. Bureau of Labor Statistics, the median income for forest and conservation workers is $23,300 annually. The median income for the top 90th percentile is $44,660 annually. As of 2010, the Department of Labor reported 13,700 forest and conservation workers employed in the United States. The field is expected to increase only one percent between 2010 and 2020, an increase of 10 jobs per year over a 10-year period. You can work as a park ranger if you have a high school diploma or GED. However, to earn higher pay, it is recommended that you earn a bachelor's degree or higher from an accredited university.

Suddenly you realize that you aren't likely to make enough money in this field to support the quality of life you desire. Now what? You must develop options! Perhaps you adjust your quality of life expectations. Maybe you will have to find a second source of income to allow you to pursue your passion. You may decide that you are better off getting a higher paying job with a liberal vacation policy in a geographic location that allows you the opportunity to fulfill your passion to enjoy the outdoors. Without additional options you're dead in the water. Again, develop options and make an informed decision sooner rather than later. Trust me…it's less mentally, emotionally, and financially costly.

2. Create a Career Map

"Believe deep down in your heart that you're destined to do great things." **Joe Paterno, Hall of Fame Football Coach, Educator, and Philanthropist**

Get online and find career mapping sites or meet with a career counselor to give you a better understanding of how to visualize what it potentially looks like to achieve your dream job in a fulfilling and exciting career. Knowing where you want to get to is an important exercise, even though we know there will be detours along the way. Work with your Pragmatic Passion Partner and then take your draft to a professional guidance counselor or career coach.

In the spring of 1982, I sat down with a sheet of lined paper and created my own map for a career in the hockey industry. I read the biographies of people who were coaches, athletic directors, and front office executives, to see the different paths they took en route to their positions. I met with my advisor Jim Kelly and my marketing academic advisor, Dr. Dave Wilson, and came up with the mapping in the photo on the next page. Next I asked Head Football Coach Joe Paterno, who at that time was the Athletic Director as well, for a letter of recommendation. I had gotten to know Coach while I was president of the Hockey Club. That letter helped me land an internship with the Pittsburgh Penguins of the NHL, which evolved into my first full-time job.

I can trace my actual career path on the map on the next page over 35 years later. If you read my biographical information you will see that after I started in the pro hockey world in sales and marketing, I crossed over to a graduate assistant coach and a head coach in college, then became an associate athletic director before crossing back over to become a vice president of an NHL team. While I never reached my top goals of a professional coach or general manager or an athletic director at a college, I got pretty darned close!

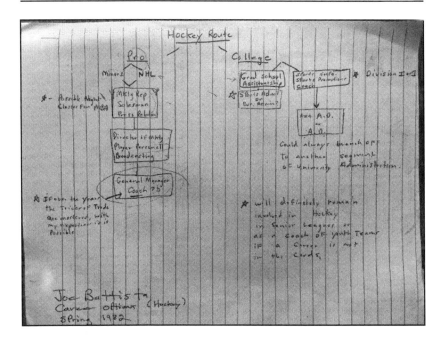

My career map created in May of 1982 that helped
me plan the next steps in my journey.

The point here is there is no one path to career success, but it
is PRAGMATIC to have a plan that is aligned with your values, interests, passions, and purpose.

You *can* figure out what you want to be when you grow up
and begin to take the steps toward that goal. You just have to
make up your mind to get started, do your research, devise a
plan, and put it into action. Inaction, apathy, and throwing a
pity party for yourself, are just excuses and won't move you
forward.

Do your research to develop options and make informed
choices and you will discover what aligns with your passion

and purpose so you'll have a better idea of what journey you want to try. Perhaps you will even decide that you want to find a purpose and career where you never really have to grow up!

"Find something that you love to do, and find a place that you really like to do it in. I found something I loved to do. I'm a mechanical engineer by training, and I loved it. I still do. My son is a nuclear engineer at MIT, a junior, and I get the same vibe from him. Your work has to be compelling. You spend a lot of time doing it." **Ursula Burns, Former CEO of Xerox**

Real Life 101: Making Tough, But Informed Choices

Tom Kozlik was an outstanding student and a hard-nosed college hockey player finishing up his junior year when he came to visit me in my coach's office. We had a very emotional conversation and "Koz" courageously and wisely told me he had decided not to play during his senior year. Most people were amazed that a young man would pass up the opportunity to be a team captain of his college hockey team during his senior year on a team poised to contend for a National Championship.

Why did he do it? To be a teaching assistant for a Political Science class and to focus on school with the goal of gaining acceptance into the University of Pennsylvania's prestigious Fels Institute of Government. We went on to win a national title that year and one of the first congratulatory calls I received was from Tom. During the call he said, "Coach I have some great news of my own. I was accepted into graduate school at Penn!"

Today Tom is a Managing Director and Municipal Strategist at PNC Financial Services and an instructor at the Fels Institute of Government at Penn. He is a periodic expert guest on national television shows on CNN, Bloomberg, and Fox. We both won a championship that spring. Tom's was acceptance into a prestigious program at an Ivy League institution.

Another former hockey player, Andrew Strasser, hailed from Sydney, Nova Scotia and followed in his father's footsteps to pursue an engineering degree in college. As a freshman, "Strass" battled homesickness, adapting to a new country and a campus larger than his hometown, until he found his academic purpose. Unhappy as an engineering student, he met with our academic advisor Ruth Hussey, who helped guide him through his exploration of potential career choices.

Everything turned around for Strass as he learned what his real passion was, and his confidence grew. He achieved on the ice (becoming team captain) and became the first paid assistant coach in our program's history. And he did all of this while earning a Ph.D. in Bio-Behavioral Health, which allowed Strass to pursue his interests in behavioral and biological sciences that he uncovered through undergraduate courses.

Dr. Strasser is now a Research Associate Professor of Behavioral Health in Psychiatry at the Perelman School of Medicine at the University of Pennsylvania, happily married to a fellow Penn State alum, and continues to coach sports, including hockey. It was Andrew's courage and willingness to address his situation, to seek out professional assistance to develop better career options, and his ability to make an informed choice that set him on a path to personal and professional success.

3. Education Options: College Is Not for Everyone (At Least Not At 18!)

"Young adults are graduating with the equivalent of monthly home mortgage payments, but without the house! They end up in retail jobs while trying to find work in their fields." **Ken "The Spice Man" Snyder, Ambassador for the Foundation for Free Enterprise Education**

Why do some kids go to college at 18? Because they don't know what they want to do, so they hope they will figure it out while in college. Does that sound very pragmatic, given the high cost of college education today?

It would be a perfect world if everyone had the same academic capabilities and sailed through vigorous college studies with straight A's and had a thorough expertise of their subject matter. Indeed, it would be ideal if after tipping their caps at graduation, every college graduate proceeded to slide into a high-paying job where they applied their academic knowledge on a daily basis. But do not fool yourself—we do not live in that world. Some young people are just not cut out for the academic strain of college at age 18. Some people attend college for four or five years and end up with the equivalent of a high-priced vacation with parties, sports, spring break trips, and they may or may not even graduate. Some actually receive a degree, but without really getting an education, as they put in a minimal effort necessary to earn what can too often be a meaningless diploma.

Pragmatic Point: Consider a "gap year" if you have not identified any interests, passions, or purpose.

For those who cannot currently bear the weight of a college workload and are unsure how to navigate through the myriad of options, a gap year may be the answer. A true, developmental gap year is not a time to goof off, binge watch some TV series, or backpack through Europe for the heck of it. It is a time to get a job, perhaps in a service industry that will allow you to save some money and get more serious and pragmatic about your future. You gain maturity from having to show up at work, go through training, be held accountable, get a paycheck, pay taxes, and problem solve in the real world. You can use this time to volunteer, job shadow, interview experts in the field, and go onto career exploration websites.

It is important to remember that just because your path deviates from the conventional wisdom, does not mean you are "defective" or "unsuccessful."

"To be competitive in the 21st century economy, every student needs career preparation, general education, and applied technical skills." **Dr. Kevin Fleming, Author of the Bestseller (Re)Defining the Goal**

While participating in a training program at Huntingdon Area School District, I engaged School Superintendent Fred Foster in a discussion about Pragmatic Passion. He recommended I watch Dr. Kevin Fleming's animation video called "Success in the New Economy," which is a refreshing look at planning for your future. This video is a MUST see for anyone looking to get a competitive advantage in the new 21st century marketplace. Dr. Fleming is a kindred spirit who gives very pragmatic advice about the importance of getting your post-secondary options in order. As he says, "You can't afford the time or money to get this wrong." He emphasizes that the "college is for everyone" advice, especially at 18, is flawed. Dr. Fleming believes there are numerous routes that will set you up to make a good living.

The reality is that college may not be for everyone and incurring ridiculous amounts of debt going to college without any notion or your interests, strengths, passions, or purpose, is not very pragmatic! There are outstanding technical and vocational careers that are an avenue many should at least consider, especially given a national shortage in skilled labor. There are high paying careers that don't require a 4-year degree that may better align with your skill set. Careers as a dental hygienist, construction manager, HVAC technician, electrician, plumber, medical technician, and more will allow you to enjoy a career with great benefits and very competitive salaries with some starting at $35,000 a year, averaging $60,000 a year, and allowing the more experienced folks to make over $100,000 annually.

We have significant gaps in the number of Americans earning both college and trade/technical degrees compared with the number of jobs that will need to be filled. This is due in part to the large number of Baby Boomers set to retire in the next decade. That spells OPPORTUNITY.

While it is true that college graduates earn more money and have a higher standard of living over the long haul, not everyone is meant to go to college. This is especially true considering the staggering amounts of college debt that exist today. The key is to pre-position yourself for success!

Here are just a few "non-traditional" and "non-linear" educational and career paths to consider:

- High School (HS) grad to Military to College on the GI bill

- HS to Gap Year to Community College to transfer to a 4-year school

- HS to Post Graduate Prep School to 4-year College or University

- HS to the workforce to Community College to College or University

- HS to Trade School to Work to Night School for Associate Degree

- GED to Work to Trade School

- HS to College ROTC to Military to Workforce

- HS to a Large University to Gap Year Transfer to a Small College

- HS to a Small College to Gap Year to Transfer to a Large University

Pragmatic Point: According to Tradesmen International, there is a severe shortage of applicants for well-paying skilled labor jobs, and that is predicted to grow through 2024.

Home Depot CEO Craig Menear announced in March of 2018 that his company would be donating $50 million to train 20,000 people in the trades over the next decade to help fill in the gap. Again, this spells opportunities that too often you may miss because of the "sea of sameness" that everyone must go to college to be successful.

Real Life 101: A Long and Winding Road to a Vocational Career

In February of 2017, Scott Good, owner of Goodco Mechanical, and I went to Ken Hassinger's HVAC class at the Central Pennsylvania Institute of Science and Technology (CPI). We were there to discuss career development and the importance of "soft skills" in the job market.

But Brian Price, a 27-year-old recent graduate from CPI's HVAC class, upstaged us. Brian's biological father was never a part of his life and Brian had dropped out of school at age 14 due to his mother's substance abuse issues. "I had to quit school to work just so we could eat," Brian said. "Mom came

to me with her problems. My mother was my anti-drug poster. I chose to go a different path."

Brian's first jobs were at a local restaurant and as a delivery
driver for another, where he had to lie about his age just to
start working. While working, Brian made time to earn his
GED. Then, he picked up part-time work as a laborer at a local car wash. At age 18, Brian enrolled at CPI, where he tried
nursing but didn't like it. He dropped out and did skilled
trade work, mostly in construction. He was fortunate to get a
good job in the natural gas business, but it only lasted three
years and then he was laid off when his industry hit a down-
turn.

He could have made more money on unemployment than
from working, but he didn't want to live off the government.
His life took a positive turn when he got engaged to an old
friend from his teenage years, Janelle. With a new relationship and family, he knew he needed a career change. "I was
thinking of going to IT school but Janelle said, 'You are happiest working with your hands,' so I listened to her advice."

Brian went back to CPI and enrolled in the HVAC program
after qualifying for grant money and getting a reasonable student loan. He graduated in one year and started full-time
with Goodco just four days after graduation. Brian began as a
residential HVAC installer and was assigned to a great mentor. When his mentor relocated, Brian had such high ratings
that Scott trusted him with the group leader position.

I asked Brian if there was an "a-ha moment" when all his values and attitudes kicked in, or did he always have such a pragmatic approach to work and life?

"Not any one moment. I have had my share of ups and downs," he said. "Taking pride in my work, having self-worth, being optimistic, and being practical are part of who I am. You can't just crawl in a corner and find your safe space. You have to tackle challenges. Sitting around moping and complaining is not me. I don't want pity. I have overcome a lot and I am happily married and have great kids. We are very content."

We hear about people who are living as "entitled dependents" and milking the system. Brian is living proof of the good that can come from taking charge of your life.

4. Career Options: Knowing When It's Time to Move On

Deciding to disrupt and change paths in life is not reserved only for high school and college-aged kids. If you are stuck in a passionless, stagnant career, it is important to recognize the signs, determine your options and make informed decisions *before* you act. Drawing from the decision-making advice in Objective 1, decide if this career can still get you to your end goal. If it cannot, then set a time limit for when to take action and switch jobs to pursue the life you want. Remember to balance your emotions properly and think objectively; consider the Eisenhower-Covey Decision Matrix!

In his book, ***When to Jump: If the Job You Have Isn't the Life You Want***, Mike Lewis suggests that there are four phases for knowing when to leave a job:

1. Listen to the little voice in your head telling you to consider doing something about your idea.

2. Make a plan – it means you have acted upon the idea, drafting more tangible steps.

3. Let yourself be lucky – you've prepared enough, now it's time to commit to the jump!

4. Don't look back – you put everything into this new journey, keep moving forward!

In taking these steps, you can pursue your passion while remaining pragmatic. Put thought into your plan and make it bulletproof so that you have a way to support yourself during this career change. Keep the 10-10-10 Rule in mind. How will you feel about this decision in 10 minutes? 10 weeks? 10 years? If the answer is positive, then pursue this new path enthusiastically and passionately!

Can you afford to take time off to go back and get a Master's Degree or a Ph.D.? Have you factored in the lost wages into your calculations? Will it really advance your career? To be pragmatic, you must be able to answer these tough questions before you move on to new challenges.

Pragmatic Point: It's easier to jump when you have a parachute and have gone through the proper training. So it is with deciding to change jobs or careers.

Chapter 6 Summary:

1. The decision-making process

2. How to set goals that are based in reality

3. Making educational and career decisions that make sense

Answer the questions below:

1. When have you made an impulsive decision that ended in a poor outcome?

_____

_____

_____

2. What decision-making tools could you have used to gather better information that could have resulted in a better conclusion for you?

_____

_____

_____

3. Describe a time in your life when you set unrealistic goals based on bad assumptions?

_____

_____

_____

4. Describe a time in your life when you set realistic, achievable goals that led to an informed decision?

_____

_____

_____

5. How could a coach, mentor, or subject expert assist you with a professional development plan?

_____

_____

_____

6. What resources do you need to help you make a possible career decision?

_____

_____

_____

"Inability to make decisions is one of the principal reasons executives fail. Deficiency in decision-making ranks much higher than lack of specific knowledge or technical know-how as an indicator of leadership failure." **John C. Maxwell, Author of The 360-Degree Leader**

Chapter 7
Nurture

"Every day you have the opportunity to learn and experience something and someone new. Seize the opportunity. Learn and experience everything you can and use it to change the world."

**Rodney Williams, Technology
Entrepreneur and CEO of LISNR**

Chapter 7 Objectives:

1. Grow your mind – grow your possibilities

2. Networking that really counts

3. Personal money management is a key to a joyful and fulfilling life

4. Recommended readings

You have now reached the seventh and final Pragmatic Passion Core Principle. It might be worth going back and reading the Chapter 1-6 summaries as a refresher since the first six principles feed into this chapter.

So, what do I mean by "nurture"? According to the *Oxford Dictionary,* nurture is "the process of caring for and encouraging the growth or development of someone or something." That "someone" is you first, so that you can in turn provide support and encouragement for others as a servant leader.

One of my best mentors ever was one of my first supervisors, Charles "Vance" McCullough. Vance often told me stories of what it was like being an Army Ranger during the Vietnam War. He taught me a saying that he learned that I would never forget. "Each one reach one. Each one teach one." Vance was as passionate as he was intense. He spent a lifetime trying to make other people better. I am fortunate that he was able to reach out to me and most importantly, to teach me. That is nurture at its finest.

Having a growth mindset means developing a commitment to professional and personal development. It means to nurture life-long learning by developing a daily ritual to learn something new or to intentionally review important aspects of your vocation and avocations on a regular basis. It is making a conscious choice to share your knowledge and wisdom with others. You must now simply make the commitment to follow through.

Tom Peters, author of the best selling business book, *In Search of Excellence* says, "Management is about arranging and telling. Leadership is about nurturing and enhancing."

The rest of this chapter is dedicated to nurturing you and your future.

Objective 1: Grow Your Mind - Grow Your Possibilities

"It's kind of fun to do the impossible." **Walt Disney, Founder and President of The Walt Disney Company**

During my time as a coaching certification instructor for USA Hockey, I would frequently start off my sessions with the following statement: "The day you think you know everything about this game and don't think you can learn any more, please do us all a favor and stop coaching. You must never stop learning as there is always something new you can learn if you are willing to open your mind."

The challenge with continued learning is that some people never grasped how to learn in the first place. I believe improving your study skills should be a priority and it should be given a higher priority in our public education system. Take the necessary steps to improve your learning skills and then seek out schools and workplaces that will embrace what you have to offer them.

I believe education is the currency of the future. I believe a revolution is coming in the way in which you learn, how it's delivered, and where you will be when you are learning (hint: anywhere that Wi-Fi is available!). The rate at which technology (and information dispersal) is changing and its use in our lives is ever increasing. To achieve success, regardless of how you define it, you must embrace technology and that means committing to a life of learning and professional development.

And the best way to embrace technology and education is to know why you're learning in the first place. Long-time friend, John Herington, is a corporate trainer and owner of Personal Budgets by John. In a recent discussion about teaching people basic budgeting skills, he talked about the fact that people's ability to complete a task improves if they know the purpose and how it applies to everyday life. "How many times in school did you ask yourself, why do I need to learn this stuff? If we understand the purpose, we are more likely to complete the task."

The goal is to never stop learning. Use your Pragmatic Passion mindset and continue to develop your skills, abilities, and thought-processes, so you can open your mind and your possibilities.

Pragmatic Point: A 2017 U.S. Dept. of Labor report predicts that 65% of today's youth will eventually have jobs that have yet to be created.

1. Learn to Love to Learn!

"Where you are 5 years from now is directly related to the people you meet, and the books you read." **Lou Holtz, Legendary NCAA Football Coach and Analyst**

If you want to gain confidence and courage to grow your opportunities in life, then continue to grow your mind. You should do everything you can to develop an insatiable appetite for learning. The future will be all about developing a skill set that allows for versatility, flexibility, collaboration, innovation, and an entrepreneurial spirit. If you commit to constant and continuous learning, then you will put yourself in a position to always be relevant and marketable to future employers. You will be one step ahead of the competition in creating the ideas and innovations that will appeal to consumers. You will be a better, healthier person, spouse, parent, leader, mentor, and friend if you continue to grow your mind.

Let me expand upon Coach Holtz's quote…**your future also depends on the conferences you attend, the webinars you watch, the online courses you take, and podcasts that you hear.**

My game plan for attending conferences, seminars, retreats, and training sessions is as follows: Arrive early and try to meet the speakers. Stay afterward and ask them meaningful questions. Even if you don't get to ask questions, many times you will hear great ideas that they are sharing with others. A small nugget you pick up or a short meeting with the speaker could turn out to be a seminal moment for you.

Today there is no excuse for not continuing to learn and grow, as there are so many resources available and different ways to embrace continuing education. Many of those resources are free and at your disposal by going to a public library for reading materials, DVDs, and computers for you to browse the internet for free content or pay for service programs.

One of my former team captains at Penn State, Dr. Mark Konchar, is a Senior Vice President and Chief of Innovation at Balfour Beatty, a global leader in engineering and construction. He gave me the book *Humanizing the Education Machine: How To Create Schools That Turn Disengaged Kids Into Inspired Learners* by Rex Miller. Rex and his co-authors challenge the status quo in education by highlighting programs that are thriving from inner city schools to the most affluent communities. Co-Author Brian Cahill says, "We can't teach students of the 21st Century with 19th Century methods. The pace of change is increasing exponentially. Learning must include the ability to adapt, collaborate, and bounce back in a world of flux."

With the advent of online alternatives to higher education like MOOCs (Massive Open Online Courses), Khan Academy, and Coursera, it is hard to predict where the future of education is heading. It's a safe bet that at least a portion of all learning will be done virtually, perhaps in a hybrid in-person/online manner. Yes folks, the "Google Revolution" is finally replacing the "Guttenberg Revolution" and the sooner those of us that are "Digital Immigrants" accept this, the better we will communicate with younger generations.

With the changing job market and changes brought about by technology, you must think in terms of developing your skills and knowledge and having a growth mindset. The foundation you build with your new skills, traits, and competencies is more important than ever. Employers will want to see that you can learn new skills and can roll with change.

"Take chances, make mistakes. That's how you grow. Pain nourishes your courage. You have to fail in order to practice being brave." **Mary Tyler Moore, Actress, Producer, Businesswoman**

2. Embrace Technology by Controlling It, Not Letting It Control You!

To avoid information overload, ask yourself if you really need to know about some random news report or the latest social happenings from your friends, and do you need to know it right now? Limit or even turn off superfluous news, sports, and entertainment alerts. Every unnecessary "ding" or vibration is an interruption causing you to lose focus. Do you really need the 24-hour news, sports, and weather reports for you to achieve success in your life? Or are they distractions that are keeping you from deliberate and intentional work toward your goals?

Pragmatic Point: Under normal circumstances at school and at work, you should schedule specific times in your day to check your digital devices. For example, only check texts and emails after breakfast, just before or after lunch, and just before or after dinner. The exception is if you must be reached immediately because of an event or if your job requires constant real-time communication.

It's easy to get sucked into meaningless online conversations with friends and even strangers in the comments section of Twitter and Facebook. Just because someone contacts you does not mean you must respond, and you certainly don't need to respond immediately. Go back to the Eisenhower-Covey Decision Matrix and ask if it's important and urgent enough that you must deal with it right now.

Personally, I've made huge mistakes over the years in my judgment with emails, texts, and Twitter. Sending emotional rants late at night without the necessary time to think through my messages, or instant messaging someone when my emotions were too high, cost me personally and professionally. I did not use a Pragmatic Passion mindset and too often reacted impulsively to stressful situations. It's important to realize that just because you can answer questions quickly doesn't mean you should answer questions without using common sense and critical thinking skills.

A Pew Research Center 2010 report on Millennials (born between 1981 and 1996) says this about this often misunderstood generation of "Digital Natives":

> They are history's first "always connected" generation. Steeped in digital technology and social media, they treat their multi-tasking hand-held gadgets almost like a body part – for better and worse. More than eight-in-ten say they sleep with a cell phone glowing by the bed, poised to disgorge texts, phone calls, emails, songs, news, videos, games, and wake-up jingles.

Everyone, including Millennials, must factor in that anyone in Generation Z (born after 1996) doesn't remember life without smartphones and social media, so it would be a mistake to ignore the cultural differences that exist between the generations.

The Gamification of learning is upon us. Video games have enchanted and captivated modern society with revenues upwards of $137.9 billion worldwide. From mobile, to PC, to consoles, the video game industry has surpassed both the music industry and movie industry combined. Online access is afforded 24-7 leading to controversy and questions about health and engagement of these advanced interactive digital tools.

However, Dr. Jason A. Engerman, a colleague of mine with the National Athletic and Professional Success Academy (NAPSA) and an expert in game-based education, believes the skills and knowledge that are developed by playing digital games, outweigh any negatives. He is a learning designer, philosopher, learning scientist, educational change agent, youth advocate, and playcologist. Yes, a playcologist.

His innovative work and research revolves around the use of digital media, such as games, as authentic learning tools. Jason views life as a great game, and that we humans are the players in a giant game of life. "I believe playcologists put the human element back into living a full life. Human beings sometimes have a hard time just being human and I believe we've forgotten a basic truth...We are all players!"

The advancements of technologies like video games have imposed great demands for growth and new skill sets to navigate in an ever-changing global economy. The future will be all about developing and mastering tools that allow for strategy, versatility, flexibility, an entrepreneurial spirit, collaboration, and innovation.

Dr. Jason Engerman (L), an expert in "playcology,"
with former College All-American and retired
NFL player Aaron Beasley at the National Athletic
and Professional Success Academy.
[*Courtesy of Rick Brandt*]

Objective 2: Networking That Really Counts

Business relationships are important. Personal relationships are essential. If you start with the goal of building meaningful personal relationships, then your business relationships will take care of themselves. If people know you genuinely care about them, they will more likely want a meaningful relationship to exist.

So, make it a priority to get to know people on a more personal level. How? While I am an advocate of using LinkedIn professionally and social media platforms personally, just because someone accepts your invite doesn't mean you suddenly have a meaningful relationship. While it is important to remember people's birthdays, doing something nice for them out of the blue when they least expect it would be far more impactful. Being there for them in times of need is the highest level of a meaningful relationship.

What I learned in my time in sales and in fundraising is that people do business with people, and people donate money to people. It's all about quality relationships. Sure, people may do transactional deals with you that have little or no real value, and they will write you the small check for a donation to a cause. But in order to land the bigger business deals and to close on the transformational gifts for non-profits, it is predominantly based on the strength of the relationship that has formed between parties.

Transactional Leadership focuses on management, task completion, efficiencies, and achieving a set objective to improve performance. It focuses on conventional wisdom and maintaining the status quo and day-to-day operations. It is necessary, but not sufficient, to create real change in performance.

Transformational Leadership inspires motivation and engagement of the people in your care by focusing everyone on the same vision.

1. Improve Your People Skills

Passion Point: If you want to be successful, you must intentionally improve your people skills!

How? By practicing! You can't get better with your people skills if you don't actively engage others in social and work settings. You must be intentional and deliberate in reaching out to colleagues, friends, and relatives in order to build meaningful relationships. I am referring to conversational interactions in person, by videoconferencing, or at a minimum, by phone.

And when you do engage in conversations with others, it's important to focus on the other person and remember the key values and characteristics that make up a meaningful, authentic relationship. Values like: trust, courtesy, mutual respect, empathy, dignity, and forgiveness. Characteristics like: smiling a lot, having a positive attitude, saying thank you, avoiding gossip, and actively listening.

In addition, bringing these values and characteristics to each conversation you have, can open doors to career advancements, professional development opportunities, assignment of key projects, and even a raise! Remember, if you want to build truly authentic relationships, then you must make a concerted effort.

On the flip side, there are specific reasons why relationships fail. Here are the big ones to avoid:

- Lack of respect for others (egocentric, selfish priorities)

- Lack of communication skills (hearing, but not listening)

- Lack of personal engagement in relationships (too much automation, too task driven)

- Lack of psychological safety (trust issues, too much gossip)

- Lack of empathy (context and perspective)

- Lack of confidence (micromanagement and skepticism)

In order to improve our people skills and build better relationships, we must combat these traits and be intentional about improving our ability to understand, to communicate, to respect, and to work with others.

2. Build Better Relationships by Using the 7 C's

"There is a 'win-win' solution to just about everything." **Joe Battista**

We can all work better together by using the 7 C's: civility, compassion, collaboration, creativity, communication, critical thinking, and compromise.

So, before you start a verbal joust with someone you disagree with, or before you jump into a heated conversation online or offline, educate yourself first (and double-check your facts), so you can understand the context and empathize with those you are about to critique.

This can be done in several ways. You can educate yourself online (utilizing reputable sources, not with social media) or by reading books. You can educate yourself by attending classes or seminars. And, the best way to educate yourself so you can form a well-rounded opinion about any topic is to spend time with people who have the opposite point of view you currently have.

Go spend time in an inner-city school. Go visit a manufacturing plant in the middle of the country. Go visit a high-tech firm. Go spend a week in another country. Go to a coal-mining town. Meet with the owner of a small business. Go to your state capital and talk with a senator or representative. Meeting with people who take the opposite viewpoint of yours will give you a new perspective and perhaps will help you have a better understanding, so you can better relate to their issues before you decide to hammer them without context.

Do you really want to make a difference with your relationships? Then begin to prepare for how to respectfully work with those who have an opposing view. It's fine to have differences, but the angry and disrespectful nastiness being spewed by uneducated people must give way to civility, compassion, collaboration, cooperation, and compromise for the greater good. Here are a few suggestions to work on relationships with those with a different view:

- Close your eyes, take a deep breath, and say to yourself, "Peace, be still." It doesn't always work, but give it a try.

- Be the first to forgive and be willing to be forgiven.

- Quit talking via social media or text. Call and say, "Let's grab a coffee and talk."

- Learn to say, "I'm sorry that we disagree. I will try better to understand your position."

- "We appear to be at a standstill. How about we sleep on it and continue the discussion when we calm down and can be more dispassionate?"

- Use active listening and use it more often than you speak.

- Seek to understand first before going off on a rant you may regret.

Let me be clear. None of this means you must give up your stance (though your viewpoint may adapt). Just be open and willing to listen to other people's opinions and find a good solution when differences come up. And do it with civility, compassion, collaboration, creativity, communication, critical thinking, and compromise.

Objective 3: Nurture Your Dreams by Learning to Nurture Your Money

"Be a good steward of your money so your dreams can come true!" **Joe Battista**

Regardless of your personal definition of success, pragmatic and proper money management is necessary to achieve and sustain even the most modest of dreams. Do you feel comfortable with money management and financial literacy? If not, I suggest making this a top priority, so you can nurture your dreams and your future.

People tend to spend money impulsively and frivolously because they believe they are entitled. We convince ourselves that we "deserve" to take vacations even if it means putting it on a credit card and paying it off at some ridiculous interest rate (often as much as 24%!). I know people who financed fancy vacations they really couldn't afford and are still paying them off ten years later.

The better understanding you have of money management, the more confidence you'll have to make your dreams come true. People will impulsively go to concerts, sporting events, and on vacations and spend excessively on cars, clothes, and eating out without ever considering the costs. In too many cases they are living a "status lifestyle" beyond their means just to impress people. Then they say, "I just don't have any money" when it's time to go to conferences and professional development training, get a degree or advanced degree, learn a trade, or to fund their new business idea.

"Consumerism is using money you haven't earned, to buy things you don't need, to impress people you don't like."
Syndicated Humorist Robert Quillen

While money management is not an area of expertise for me, thankfully I learned the importance of understanding the basics in my twenties. I grew up in a blue collar Italian family where we never talked about family finances and basic money fundamentals were not taught in my K-12 schools. I didn't have a trust fund, nor will I receive an inheritance from my parents. I learned from a former hockey player's parents who worked in the financial industry; by taking a continuing education course called "Money 101" (more valuable than many classes I was forced to take in college); by reading a book called *Your Wealth Building Years* by Adriane Berg; by working with a financial coach; and through good old trial and error.

So, while I won't give you any hot stock tips (those usually don't work so well anyway!), I will do my best to inspire you to meet with a financial planner, take a class or two, read a book, and spend deliberate time learning at least the fundamentals of money management.

Here are some timeless philosophies to help you get started.

"Save For A Rainy Day."

When you are out of work, your savings will work for you. The conventional financial wisdom is that you should have 3-6 months of liquid assets available in case of an emergency brought on by downsizing or a major health crisis. Most people have been brainwashed into believing they must have the latest smartphone, a status car, a bigger house than they need, access to more multi-media channels than they will ever have time to watch, and a $4 or $5 cup of coffee every day. While I believe that you should enjoy the money you make, I believe you should save your money before you spend your money. That way you'll have a safety net if things don't go your way.

"Live Within Your Means."

I am constantly on my own kids about spending less than you make and practicing "delayed gratification." Unfortunately, they can't follow our federal government's example, which has managed to spend us into a national debt we may never see resolved. Don't buy "wants" when you can't afford "needs."

"A Penny Saved Is A Penny Earned."

In a commencement speech at Lock Haven University in 2016, Dr. Thomas "Doc" Sweitzer, Executive Director of the Campaign Group, gave the class this advice: "The best thing you could do when starting a new job is to immediately start an IRA. The pension plans your parents and grandparents had will not be around. And by the way, playing the lottery is not a retirement plan! Your odds of getting struck twice by lightning are greater than winning the Powerball."

Social Security, if still around, may require a higher starting age, less money per payout, may be taxed at a higher rate, or not be available to those who have a net worth above a certain amount in the future. So do yourself a favor, learn how to save for retirement and start doing it now.

"Never Stop Learning About Money."

When the Penn State players I coached would graduate, I gave them a book about money management. For most of my coaching tenure, I gave out *Your Wealth Building Years: Financial Planning for 18-38 Year Olds* by Adriane Berg. When that went out of print, I switched to *The Millionaire Next Door* by Thomas J. Stanley and *The Automatic Millionaire* by David Bach.

All of these books preached similar philosophies about a disciplined approach to spending, saving, and investing for the long haul. In fact, you learn that most millionaires live very simple lifestyles and accumulate lasting wealth because they are pragmatic with their money, passionate about saving and living beneath their means, and disciplined enough to follow through.

A few years ago, my son Jonathon and I ran into one of my former players, Teague Willits-Kelley, in town. Teague told him that reading *The Automatic Millionaire* was one of the best things he ever did. He thanked me for presenting that to him at his senior banquet and I could not have asked for a better endorsement for my own son to hear!

"If It Sounds Too Good To Be True, It Probably Is."

One of my favorite business books is ***Beware the Naked Man Who Offers You His Shirt*** by New York Times Best Selling author Harvey Mackay. He essentially describes the saying, "If it sounds too good to be true, it probably is."

Think about Bernie Madoff, who defrauded thousands of educated, wealthy investors out of $19 billion. That's right, billions. It was actually $65 billion in fictitious gains that his clients believed they had earned but in reality, it was the largest

Ponzi scheme in history. There is plenty of "swamp land in Florida" and "gold in them thar hills," too.

Another case worth reading about is white-collar criminal John Ackah Blay-Miezah, who along with the Prime Minister of Ghana, promised investors a 1,000 percent return on their investments. Does that sound pragmatic to you? It's hard to believe so many smart people fell for that one, too.

"Trust But Verify."

Not every con artist is after millions. There are a lot of crooks trying to scam regular citizens as well. There will always be evil in the world and people who will prey on the naïveté that makes good people do strange things when influenced by greed. Be cautious when things either seem "too good to be true" or when someone you didn't personally seek out to purchase from asks you for money. Trust, but verify.

"There's No Such Thing as a Free Lunch."

This is a hard one for many people to understand, especially in this age of "entitlement." Every time I hear a politician make an outrageous statement promising unrealistic outcomes simply to secure a vote, it gets my blood boiling. I am equally upset that so many people fall for them.

I am an ardent supporter of higher education if it's done properly. However, does the talk of "free college tuition for everyone" sound practical to you? Where is that money going to come from? Taxpayers. You, me, and those who don't even realize they will get dinged. So those of you who are 25 and under who are basing your future votes on that unrealistic promise, remember you will be one of those taxpayers for 40 plus years paying for others 4-5 years of "free" education.

Pragmatic Point: Don't measure success just in dollars and cents, material goods, and "status."

I believe we should make basic consumer math skills and financial literacy a mandatory part of the curriculum at least a few semesters during K-12 classes and at post-secondary colleges and trade schools. So many of society's problems can be traced back to people's poor money habits.

Pragmatic Passion's Basic Money Rules Checklist:

1. Create a budget and stick to it.

2. Practice delayed gratification. Don't spend what you don't have, especially on frivolous "stuff."

3. Don't live a "status lifestyle," have the courage to avoid peer pressure to keep up with the Joneses.

4. Find a credible, certified financial planner, and research whether to pay by the hour or fee based.

5. Use a "pay yourself first" strategy. Direct deposit a percentage of your paycheck to savings and investments.

6. Have 3-6 months of your monthly expenses in emergency savings (in case of job loss, medical bills, etc.).

7. Put away at least what your company will match in your retirement programs.

8. Create a will, research and purchase the right types of insurance, and keep all your personal records and documents in a safe place.

9. Put money in investments that you fully understand until you learn more about financial markets.

10. Avoid "get rich quick" schemes and stop buying lottery tickets. Neither really work.

Objective 4: Recommended Reading

Here is a very short list of some of the books I would recommend that have made a lasting impression on me. A longer list, including a short review and comments on why I found each particular book a worthwhile read, are available by going to **www.PragmaticPassion.com/bookresources**.

I would also recommend you consider a service like Soundview's "Executive Book Summaries" or Audible.com both of which offer written and audible summaries of books to save time.

- *Good to Great* by Jim Collins
- *Inside the Magic Kingdom: Seven Keys to Disney's Success* by Tom Coleman
- *Dig Your Well Before You're Thirsty* by Harvey MacKay

- *Swim with the Sharks Without Being Eaten Alive* by Harvey MacKay

- *Your Gut is Still Not Smarter Than Your Head* by Kevin Clancy and Peter C. Krieg

- *Performance Appraisals That Work* by Corey Sandler & Janice Keefe

- *1001 Ways to Reward Employees* by Bob Nelson

- *Grit* by Angela Duckworth

- *Leading with the Heart: Successful Strategies for Basketball, Business, and Life* by Mike Krzyzewski

- *Fake Work* by Brent Peterson and Gaylan Nielson

- *Death by Meeting* by Patrick Lencioni

- *Silos, Politics, and Turf Wars* by Patrick Lencioni

- *The Five Dysfunctions of a Team* by Patrick Lencioni

- *Tribe Of Mentors* by Tim Ferriss

- *Strengthsfinder 2.0 From Gallup* by Don Clifton

- *Caught Between a Dream and a Job* by Delatorro McNeall II

- *Your Career Planner* by Cheryl Bonner and Susan Musich

- *Going for the Gold: How the U.S. Won at Lake Placid* by Tim Wendel

- *The Games Do Count: America's Best and Brightest on the Power of Sports* by Brian Kilmeade

- *Coaching* by Ralph J. Sabock & Michael D. Sabock

There are a lot more, but this is a good place to stop. I have read a few of these books more than once. With others, I refer back to for quotes, solutions, and ideas.

For more book recommendations go to **www.PragmaticPassion.com/bookresources**.

Chapter 7 Objectives:

1. Grow Your Mind – Grow Your Possibilities

2. Networking That Really Counts

3. Nurture Your Dreams by Learning to Nurture Your Money

4. Recommended Readings

Hopefully you now understand the importance of the need to nurture yourself and others by being a life-long learner, building real relationships, and handling your finances. Answer the following questions to help you develop options and make informed choices.

1. If time and cost were not a factor, what classes would you take today and why?

_____

_____

_____

2. What is the last book you read cover to cover?

_____

_____

_____

3. What books would you put on your reading list?

_____

_____

_____

4. What webinars would you like to watch?

_____

_____

_____

5. What podcasts would you like listen to?

_____

_____

_____

6. What relationships in your life need more of your attention?

_____

_____

_____

7. What can you do to improve the most important relationships in your personal and professional lives?

_____

_____

_____

8. Do you have a budget? Do you have a will? Do you have a personal money management plan?

_____

_____

_____

"A mind that is stretched by new experiences can never go back to its old dimensions." **Oliver Wendell Holmes, Jr., Supreme Court Justice**

Section Three

Get It Done!

Chapter 8
Our Dream Comes True

"You see things; you say, 'Why?' But I dream
things that never were; and I say, 'Why not?'"

**George Bernard Shaw, Author
and Nobel Prize Winner**

Would you look at that? We just got through all seven Principles of Pragmatic Passion and we made it out in one piece. Not so hard, right? This book contains examples of all these fantastic people whose real-life stories demonstrated different aspects of Passion. So, now it's time to talk about how one of my biggest, boldest dreams actually came true. And it only took 35 years!

The story of how a lifelong dream of mine, and hundreds of other hockey enthusiasts, became a reality is what inspired me to create this Pragmatic Passion Program. I hope it will inspire you.

In 1978 I was a wide-eyed freshman arriving at University Park, PA for college. I was scared and uncertain of my future, but the one thing I had was my passion for hockey and hope that the rumors of a new ice arena being built and a move to

NCAA Division I status was really in the works. On my third day on campus, that bubble burst. It was announced that the old "Ice Pavilion," built in 1955, was going to be turned into an indoor track and turf practice facility for football *before* construction would begin on the rumored new arena. Worse, it looked like the hockey club program would be put on hiatus. Not quite the welcome to Penn State I had expected.

The hockey program was saved mainly through the herculean efforts of Vance McCullough, Professor Bob Hettema, and Club President and Team Captain Jerry Fry. A temporary outdoor rink was built and for the next two years my teammates and I would skate outdoors (weather permitting), play street hockey in our Intramural Building, and travel two hours by van to Mechanicsburg, PA for occasional practices and all home games. The "Icers," as we were known at that time, were a dedicated, passionate bunch.

Despite the hardships, our team won the Mid-Atlantic Collegiate Hockey Conference championship my first two seasons. The group of guys I had the privilege to call teammates are still among my closest friends from college and regularly return for alumni functions. Construction began on the new arena in late 1979 and it was completed in January 1981, in time for the spring term of my junior year. But given the harsh economic times, the project was scaled back from its original 4,500 seats to just 1,075 seats. With that decision, our hopes of becoming a NCAA varsity sport were dashed.

Pragmatic Point: If you are a high school or post-secondary student, get involved in school clubs and organizations. If you are a parent, encourage your kids to do so. Choose one, maybe two, and try to earn an officer's position. Involvement in clubs and internships is essential to differentiate you from others.

It was my time as a player and officer in the Hockey Management Association (HMA) where my hands-on experiences helped me in my early career when I was in sales and marketing for the Pittsburgh Penguins (remember what my assessments predicted?). At 22, I started coaching the Junior Penguins. In my role as the Penguins Amateur Hockey Director, I ran player and coaching clinics locally and for USA Hockey, before moving on to be an assistant coach at Kent State and then Culver Military Academy.

In 1987, I returned to Penn State, where I was hired as the assistant director of the Greenberg Indoor Ice Pavilion and as the head coach for the men's club hockey team at Penn State. For the next 19 years, I was a part of Penn State Hockey. The Icer Family, as we were known, was an amazing organization made up primarily of volunteers, boosters, the students of the HMA, sponsors, and of course, the players and their parents. So many dedicated and passionate people put their hearts and souls into producing the best non-varsity hockey program in the country. We captured six ACHA National Championships, won over 500 games, and played before a packed arena for most home games during my time as coach.

The Greenberg facility we had been using for over 25 years was adequate, but it presented a huge barrier to expanding our hockey program to NCAA status. The Ice Pavilion only seated 1,075 people, but we regularly played in front of standing room crowds of between 1,100 and 1,600 fans. We had our own local television highlight show; all the games were on the radio; and a number of players were making minor pro hockey teams. Suddenly, people began to take notice.

We also built the summer hockey camps into a solid business, running as many as seven weeks of sold out camps with a long wait list. One of the participants in the early 1990s was Michael Pegula. The Pegula name would become a household word in Happy Valley in 20 years.

Alas, Greenberg Ice Pavilion didn't have the type of amenities that catered to fans or players, such as training facilities, weight rooms, upgraded locker rooms, upgraded or premier seating for fans, and a press box. All of these amenities are vital, because they help attract talent and bring in money for your program. In order for hockey to work logistically at the Division I level, we needed to seat at least 5,000 to 6,000 fans.

In the meantime, from 1970 until 2006 there had been numerous formal proposals made to the school administration requesting an expansion of the existing facility, adding ice to the Bryce Jordan Center, or construction of a new facility and a move to NCAA varsity status for the hockey program. All those efforts failed during my time with the school. Every time it was for the same reasons:

- "There's not enough interest in hockey in Pennsylvania."

- "We don't have the budget for such a venture."

- "The current arena is too small to support NCAA hockey."

- "There are too few local high school hockey programs."

- "There is a lack of private support and funding."

Turn a "No, because"... Into a "Yes, if"

It became clear that the University could not fund this project completely for us. Either the hockey program itself would have to foot most of the bill itself (which wasn't possible given the size of the arena) or we'd need significant private support at an unprecedented level to help us out. We'd explored our options, but we were really at an impasse. In 2005 we formed a committee that proposed a private-public partnership. Eventually in 2007, a feasibility study was funded. There was a growing interest in getting the project going, but the reality was the arena and program costs were just too prohibitive. At that time, the project was estimated to cost $50 million and the largest single private gift the university had ever received was around $25 million.

I hadn't quite resigned myself to the fact that the project would never happen, but at the time I knew there were few donors who had the capacity or willingness to give the mega gift it would take to make our dream come true. Then, on a November evening in 2005, I received a phone call that would change everything.

I was getting ready to sit down for a rare in-season dinner with my family when a PSU alumnus by the name of Terry Pegula found a way to get a hold of me. He wanted to discuss hockey that night over dinner at Kelly's Steakhouse, incidentally owned by a hockey playing family in town! Terry was a very successful businessman in oil and gas and real estate, a passionate hockey fan, and a casual Icers fan. It was his son Michael who had attended our highly successful summer hockey camps on campus.

Terry cut right to the chase as we sat down for dinner. "So what's it going to take?" he asked. "$50 million," I responded, assuming that would probably end the conversation. Terry leaned back and put his hand on his chin and said, "I think I can help you with that." I sat straight up and said, "Ok, you've got my attention!" While I was thrilled at the initial discussion, everything hinged on the Pegulas either selling their company, East Resources, Inc., or taking the company public.

Over the next five years, our families would become close friends and we would meet periodically with University officials to get updates on the possibility of a gift. I had retired from coaching and was now a fundraiser for the university, which turned out to be a huge help as we worked with Terry and his wife Kim on a possible transformational gift. It looked like a sale of East Resources would happen in late 2008, but once again fate had other plans, as the stock market crashed and for the next two years the economy was mired in the Great Recession. How cruel could the "hockey gods" be? I wondered out loud.

As the economy improved, things started to heat up, and then on May 28, 2010 I saw a newsflash on the bottom of the Bloomberg Network Channel. *"Royal Dutch Shell purchases East Resources, Inc. for record $4.7 billion."* I had to rub my eyes to see if it was true. Of course, this wasn't a guarantee of anything, as nothing is done until the papers are signed. For Terry, it was the culmination of a career spent becoming one of the world's leading authorities on oil and gas exploration. It is the great American dream coming true in the story of the visionary Penn State petroleum and natural gas engineering graduate who borrowed $7,500 from his mother and a few friends to start East Resources in 1983. Coincidentally, the same year I officially completed my degree from Penn State.

The next three months were filled with excitement and anxiety as the discussions reached a climax. There was a rather scary moment for me in July when things looked like they were going to fall apart due to a communication mix up. Everything worked out in large part because an old friend saved the day by showing "the margin of excellence" and having the courage to help smooth over a scheduling misunderstanding.

On August 25, I was in Boston finishing a guided tour of Boston University's Agganis Arena by none other than Mike Eruzione, 1980 USA Hockey Team Captain. When I shook his hand to say goodbye, my last words were, "We are hoping for our own Miracle on Ice soon." Moments later, crossing Commonwealth Avenue, I received a now famous text from Terry: "jst sgnd gift agrmnt, gr8 day 4 hky in Hapy Vally!" Let me translate: "Just signed gift agreement. Great day for hockey in Happy Valley!"

This was all made possible by the largest philanthropic gift ever given to Penn State, an incredible $88 million by alumnus Terry Pegula and his wife, Kim, that was announced at a press conference in September of 2010. The gift eventually grew to $102 million and we began the two-year process of designing, planning, constructing and operating the facility.

"It's a great day for hockey in Happy Valley!" **Terry Pegula, Sept. 17, 2010**

"TEAM PEGULA" VISION

1. Build the best collegiate hockey arena in the country

2. Ensure that is has the fastest ice surface in North America

3. Create a great fan experience

4. Construct amenities that will attract top recruits

5. Provide a great facility for the entire community

Terry asked for these five objectives to be met and "Team Pegula" responded magnificently.

It all culminated with the opening of the Pegula Ice Arena on October 11, 2013 and a 4-1 victory over Army. The $91 million, state-of-the-art ice arena was built on-time and on-budget. What makes this feat even more remarkable, was that it was accomplished in the midst of a rather somber, confusing, and divisive time in the history of the University, and most certainly in intercollegiate athletics. Pegula Ice Arena became a shining light in central Pennsylvania right when Happy Valley needed it the most.

"Luck favors the prepared." **Louis Pasteur, World Renowned Scientist and Inventor**

I didn't realize it at the time, but our dream came true in large part because of what would become the seven core principles of Pragmatic Passion! The passion, persistence, and perseverance of hundreds of determined hockey enthusiasts who had a shared **purpose** and the **attitude** to keep the dream alive, who made the **sacrifices** to see it through, who provided the **servant leadership** needed to write the proposals and do the feasibility studies, the **inspiration** of the engaged alumni and boosters, the great **options** created by Team Pegula for the arena, and the **nurturing** of all the relationships over the years, culminating with the Pegulas' incredible gift.

It was a Pragmatic Passion mindset that set the stage for that moment when Terry Pegula's passion for Penn State and his vision for hockey all aligned in the fall of 2010. It was, coincidentally, 100 years after Herb Baetz and his teammates first introduced my alma mater to the sport of hockey.

"It takes a team to complete a dream." **Joe Battista**

I cannot do justice in recognizing all the people who were part of the journey, the ups and downs, the relationships, the hurdles, and ultimately the feeling of incredible achievement when the dream came true. (See the appendix).

Team Pegula became a high performing team that included Terry and Kim Pegula, their staff from East Resources, alumnus Cliff Benson, numerous University administrators, staff from the Office of Physical Plant, Intercollegiate Athletics Administration, Crawford Architects, Mortenson Construction Management Staff, the sub-contractors, and many more. The building won five major facility design and construction awards and the success of the facility and the fledgling men's and women's varsity hockey teams has been above most people's expectations.

The men's team, under Coach Guy Gadowsky and his staff, has sold out 98% of their games playing to 104% of capacity since 2013. In 2017, in just its fifth season of NCAA play, the men's team was briefly ranked #1 in the nation, won the Big Ten Championship, earned the #9 seed in its first ever NCAA Tournament, and won its first NCAA tournament game.

Oh yes, there were many naysayers along the way, internal and external to the University. Even within our own athletic department there were those who doubted we would sell out games and that the team and the arena could ever be financially viable. We proved them wrong.

Penn State Hockey became a NCAA varsity program because of a passionate purpose. It was the perfect intersection of Terry Pegula's vision, his passion for hockey and Penn State, and the preparation that had gone on for some 100 years of planning for such a time when angels, in the form of Terry and Kim Pegula, would appear.

There will always be a few critics. Some didn't like it that a gift of this magnitude went to intercollegiate athletics. It didn't. It was a gift to the community, the entire university, and the region. There are those who complained that we should have done this, and we should have done that with the building. Well, you know what? We "Dreamed big…Kept it real… And got it done!" **On time. On budget.** It's there and it's gorgeous. Those of us who had the honor and privilege of working on the project believe it is the best arena in college hockey! And we weren't the only ones, as noted in a *Penn State Newswire* story on January 25, 2018:

> Stadium Journey ranks Pegula Ice Arena No. 1 among all of North America's collegiate hockey facilities. It was the only collegiate hockey venue listed in the top 100 college facilities overall.

The atmosphere is electric, it's loud, it's fun, and it is just an amazing achievement.

Specifically for this project, the University hired consultant Marc Farha, Executive Vice President of the ICON Venue Group. Marc commented that it was wise of the University to recognize this as a special program and unique project that required innovative collaboration.

Marc said he overheard a prominent administrator say, "I have my doubts that this will be delivered on time and on budget. We have heard that story so many times before." When I interviewed Marc, he said, "That fueled me. The gauntlet was thrown down. There were so many unsung heroes on the project." When I asked Marc why this project worked so well he replied, "Collaboration. Get the right people in the room at the right time. We all understood the importance of the stewardship of the Pegula gift. This project will always be special for those of us who were there, especially given the challenges of that time. That brought us closer together as a team."

There were definitely some bumps along the way (there always will be with a transformative project) and people who don't fully realize the sacrifices that were made. They were not there during the pivotal and occasionally heated discussions about design, cost controls, operational expenses, salaries, scholarships, and scheduling. It's sometimes easy to forget those who came before us and laid the foundation.

There are even people who think the Pegulas just walked in one day and wrote a check for $102 million. As my mentor Doc Lombra is fond of saying, "Figure they know half the story at best."

Author and former sportswriter, Lou Prato, was the person who first brought it to our attention that Penn State was among the very first college teams to ever play a hockey game back in December 1909. I am more familiar with the era from 1939-1946, when varsity hockey first existed in Happy Valley.

With the completion of Pegula Ice Arena and the return of varsity hockey after 60 years, images of the heady days of Herb Baetz, George Wolbert, Johnny Dufford, Peany Gates, Larry Lightbody, Jim O'Hora, and Doc Davis danced in my head.

None of this would've been possible if…

- A group of ice enthusiasts weren't willing to play on out-door flooded tennis courts in the 40s;

- A college freshman (Roy Scott), his buddies, and a chem-istry professor (Dr. Larry Hendry) hadn't stuck out their necks in 1970 and talked the University into resurrecting hockey as a club sport;

- A former Army captain (Vance McCullough) hadn't had the vision or the leadership to "fight the good fight" in the late 70s and then establish a paid coaching position and endowment;

- A professional academic counselor (Ruth Hussey) had not been willing to become the "hockey mom" and help hundreds of kids get a shot at a PSU degree;

- A father (Joe Battista, Sr.) had not taken his sons to "stick night" at a Penguins game in the late 60s, fostering a love of the game of hockey;

- A former Division I player (Jon Shellington) with a young wife and a new job had not been willing to volunteer to coach at a critical time;

- A hockey parent (Paul Fatur) had not answered the call to reenergize the Icers booster club by raising money and interest, and if other parents and volunteers over the years had not followed suit to carry the torch;

- The parents of two Icers players (Paul and Karen Cervellero) had not stepped forward to make the lead gift to establish the initial Icers endowment;

- A local entrepreneur (Paul Silvis) had not pushed hard to put hockey on the front burner in our athletic director's mind;

- A University administrator (Peter Weiler) had not championed our cause in the halls of Old Main;

- A sports camp director (Dick Bartolomea) had not helped us create one of the most successful hockey camp operations in the country—despite the lack of a varsity team—and spent countless hours counseling an often overly-passionate former coach;

- A distinguished professor of industrial engineering (Dr. Paul Cohen) had not spent countless hours working with players, parents, boosters and students in the Hockey

Management Association to become the "Godfather" of Icers hockey;

- An old goalie (Dr. Ray Lombra), who moonlighted as an economics professor and associate dean of one of the largest colleges at PSU, had not spent the better part of the last 23 years as my "consigliore," putting up with my wild ideas, and talking me down off the ledge many times;

- A faithful wife hadn't showed up at a hockey management meeting in 1980 and stood by this crazy old hockey guy for over 30 years;

- And of course, the dream ultimately came true with the generosity of two of the most passionate hockey fans I have ever met in Terry and Kim Pegula (along with their family's support).

All of these people played important roles in the evolution of hockey at Penn State and it was their collective passion and efforts, the incredible generosity of the Pegulas, and the hard work of Team Pegula members that are ultimately responsible for this transformational accomplishment.

Personally, it was a dream 35 years in the making.

A dream that started in 1909 with Herb Baetz, was briefly realized in the 1940s by Dr. Art Davis, John Dufford, George Wolbert and their teammates, was resurrected in the 1970s in large part due to the efforts of Coach Larry Hendry, Roy Scott, Dave McCrabb, Joe McNeil, Bill Charles, Dick Merkel, and their teammates, and kept alive by Bill Proudman, Robert "Duke" Hettema, Morris Kurtz, Jerry Fry, Clayton John, Vance McCullough, Jon Shellington, Paul Fatur, Norm Hutchison, Paul and Karen Cervellero, Dick Bartolomea, Paul Silvis, Peter Weiler, Dr. Paul Cohen, Ruth Hussey, Dr. Ray Lombra, and many more.

The journey was complete. A dream, a passion, a purpose all fulfilled. I know that I will never be able to properly thank everyone who helped make "this impossible dream come true." But I will keep trying!

With passion, a purpose, and perseverance...Dreams really can still come true!

"Christening" the ice at the Building Dedication Ceremony for Pegula Ice Arena. L to R: Team Captain Tom Olczyk, Terry Pegula, and me.
[*Courtesy of Centre Daily Times*]

Opening Night at Pegula Arena October 11, 2013.
The Nittany Lions beat Army 4-1 in the first men's
hockey game before a standing-room only crowd
of 6,370. [*Courtesy of Centre Daily Times*]

Chapter 9
What Will Your Legacy Be?

"Please think about your legacy, because
you're writing it every day."

**Gary Vaynerchuck, Author of Crushing It! How Great
Entrepreneurs Build Their Business and Influence**

What is it that you want to have said about you when you are gone? Do you want people to talk about all the "stuff" you have accumulated (ever heard of Scrooge?), or do you want to be a joyful giver who leaves behind great friendships and memories and things better than you found them?

"You will never see a U-Haul behind a hearse." **Denzel Washington, Academy Award Winner and Speaker**

For the dedication ceremony of Pegula Ice Arena, we had a line in our promotional materials that simply said:

Honor The Past.
Celebrate The Present.
Roar Into The Future!

302 | Joe Battista

Honor The Past: Never forget where you come from. It's your roots, and it helps keep you grounded when you feel a little too full of yourself.

Celebrate The Present: You never know what tomorrow will bring so take the time today to say 'thank you' often and celebrate all the good in your life.

Roar Into The Future: Attack each day with passion and purpose and a desire to make a positive difference in the world.

I always preached to the members of the Penn State Hockey "Icer Family" that we had to have "The Attitude of Gratitude" and remember the need for everyone to "give back" and not just "take away." The expectations that we had for every player who came through the "Icer Family" was to give back in some positive way, whether as a volunteer coach, referee, mentor, or by helping future players get internships and jobs. Oh, and if possible, by making a philanthropic gift.

The "Icer Family" Vision Statement:
"Players, parents, boosters, sponsors, volunteers, and engaged alumni committed to represent Penn State Ice Hockey with class and dignity. Family 1st, Academics 2nd, and Hockey 3rd. We aspire to develop productive citizens who are champions on and off the ice and possess an "Attitude of Gratitude."

Passion Point: Remember to always give back. Someone has to care.

Terry Pegula and Cliff Benson would occasionally discuss the book *Half Time: Moving From Success To Significance* and the desire to positively impact many lives, even of people you may never meet. The transformational investment the Pegulas have made in Western New York with their owner-ship of the Buffalo Bills, Sabres, and Bandits, and the con-struction of the outstanding HarborCenter Facility, are just the most visible aspects of the difference they are making and the legacy they will leave behind. Of course, we can't forget The Pegula Ice Arena that bears their name in "Hockey Val-ley."

Real Life 101: A Legacy That Turns Tragedy Into Triumph

If you want heroes to inspire you, I suggest you look to real life achievers who have overcome adversity and achieved their own dreams that you won't likely read about on Insta-gram, Twitter, or see on the cover of a magazine. So here is the true story of my friend and high school classmate, Tony Lonero.

Tony was a baseball prodigy who played Olympic and NCAA Division I baseball at the highest levels, ultimately enjoying a professional baseball career in Italy. But in 2001 he was diagnosed with Multiple Sclerosis. Rather than let this disease stop him, he proved his doctors wrong by continuing to ride in cross-country bike races. In 2016, Tony decided to leave his own legacy and founded the "Non Mollare - Ride to Finish" Scholarship Fund with fellow high school classmate

Paul Dougherty. Each year at our alma mater, Penn Hills High School, two scholarships are awarded to the students who best represent the spirit of "Non Mollare" - Never Give Up! A 2013 documentary titled "Ride To Finish" tells the courageous story of Tony's battle.

"My biggest victory to date was when I was able to finish an 80-mile bicycle race a year after discovering that I had this disease. It took me 18 hours to finish this race, and when I arrived at the finish line, there was no longer anybody there. Even with that, I did not despair. I knew that I had found a way to battle Multiple Sclerosis." **Tony Lonero**

Your Next Steps...

"Knowing is not enough; we must apply.
Willing is not enough; we must do."

Johann Wolfgang von Goethe

Congratulations! You (and your Pragmatic Passion Partner) should be very proud for making it through this book. I hope it has helped you to dig deeper and learn more about what matters to you and how you can use this information to live the joyful, fulfilling, passionate, and purposeful life you have dreamed of achieving. I hope you have discovered, created, built, or helped your own Pragmatic Passion to unfold.

Now that you have completed the book it is time to reflect upon what you have learned. Try filling in the blanks and answering the questions below and on the next page, but this time using all the skills and tools you have learned during this Pragmatic Passion journey.

Values:

_____

_____

_____

Interests:

_____

_____

_____

Skills & Knowledge:

_____

_____

_____

Natural Talents/What You Do Well:

_____

_____

_____

What Others Say You Do Well:

_____

_____

_____

Concerns/Areas For Improvement:

_____

_____

_____

Passions:

_____

_____

_____

Causes:

_____

_____

_____

Quality Of Life Desired:

_____

_____

_____

Stage of Life:

_____

_____

_____

Your Personal Vision Statement:

_____

_____

_____

Now read your personal vision statement and ask yourself the following questions:

Purpose: Does it support my values, passions, and purpose?

Attitude: Will I have the proper attitude to commit to my goals and act on my purpose?

Sacrifice: Am I willing to make the sacrifices to persist and persevere along the way?

Servant Leadership: Does it serve others first and align with my servant leadership philosophy?

Inspiration: Will I be inspired to pursue my purpose with passion to "Get It Done?"

Options: Will I devote the necessary time developing the best options so I make informed choices?

Nurture: Will it nurture me so I may live a joyful, fulfilling, passionate, and purposeful life?

Look at the life you want to live through your Pragmatic Passion lenses. Apply the 7 Pragmatic Passion Principles as often as possible to all parts of your personal and professional life. It will help lead you toward achieving both personal and professional success (as you define them of course!) and to live a joyful, fulfilling, passionate, and purposeful life.

Remember that documentary about your life that you visualized back in chapter one? Well, today you have earned the right to go back and shoot new footage and make new edits!

Now it's time to write the script for your own award-winning documentary on the life you aspire to lead.

Your Pragmatic Passion Success Plan

While no plan is perfect, and all plans must be flexible, it is my belief that you must put in writing your guiding principles that will help you to live the joyful, fulfilling, passionate and purposeful life you desire.

So go to **www.PragmaticPassion.com/bookresources** and work on your **Pragmatic Passion Success Plan**.

Your Success Plan will include your Personal Vision Statement, Genie Test Results, and Career Map. Your Mentors and Coaches, Your Pragmatic Passion Advisors Team, Your Short Term, Medium Term, and Long-Term Goals. Your Physical Health Goals, Mental and Spiritual Health Goals, and Your Financial Goals.

There will be more information available to you about putting your plan together on the website along with periodic blogs, videos, and podcasts.

My final challenge to you is to put into practice "The Attitude of Gratitude" and to "give something back" to your community, your school, youth programs, church, civic organization, or charity of your choice. Whether it is time, resources, your expertise, or financial support. You are where you are today because of those who sacrificed before you and helped mentor, coach, teach, and nurture you. Take time now to say thank you.

It's your life...take charge of it and be a difference maker for the greater good to the very best of your ability!

Dream Big. Keep It Real. Get It Done!

Stay Passionate!

Appendix

"It's a great day for hockey in Happy Valley"

Terry Pegula, Sept.17, 2010

"Team Pegula"
Administration, Design and Construction of
the Award-Winning Pegula Ice Arena

There isn't time to list everyone who had a hand in the project, but a few do deserve special recognition for their roles.

The project-management team included: Rod Kirsch, Ford Stryker, Cliff Benson, Rick Kaluza, Marv Bevan, Marc Farha, Teresa Davis, Dave Joyner, David Gray, Morris Kurtz, Ben Bouma, Chris Whittemore, Nancy Doyle, Lisa Berkey, Denny Smith, Al Karosas, and their respective support staffs.

The design team included: David Murphy, Joe Corvaia, and Stacey Jones From Crawford Architects, Allen Kachel of Bohlin-Cywinski-Jackson, and Penn State design team led by Gordon Turow and Dave Zhengut.

The Mortenson construction-management team included: Jim Yowan, Derek Cunz, Gene Hodge, Jason and Heidi Brown,

Steve Laurila, Brendan Moore, Alex Brown, Roshan Alex, Shane Marshall, Sam Thayer, Kendall Neilson, Nick Kantor, Brian Nahas, Kyle Guenther, and all the subcontractors and their staffs.

The "Frozen Five" committee (staffing, student services, arena operations, marketing and fundraising, and finances) included Rick Kaluza, Mark Bodenschatz, Mark Sherburne, Greg Myford, and yours truly. A special thank you to Guy Gadowsky, Men's Hockey Head Coach, and Josh Brandwene, Women's Head Coach, and their respective staffs for their patience and input during the construction of Pegula Arena.

I would be remiss if I didn't mention the important roles that Al Horvath, Peter Weiler, Paul Silvis, Graham Spanier, Tim Curley, the Penn State Board of Trustees, and others played during the formative time of the project. Special thanks to our colleagues at Big Ten institutions (especially Michigan, Michigan State, Minnesota, Wisconsin, and Notre Dame), Miami of Ohio, Boston University, Boston College, Minnesota-Duluth, and the Sabres, Penguins, and Flyers of the NHL.

Acknowledgments

This book would not have been written or completed without editor-publisher Weston Lyon. His tremendous patience and guidance throughout this process is deeply appreciated. Weston said it best at one of our meetings. "We have become friends first and foremost." I enjoy talking with my friend and have become inspired by his "Pragmatic Passion" in all he does.

The editorial assistance of my wife, Heidi, Cheryl Bonner, Steve Kipp, Al Stewart, and Marty Wolff has been invaluable. I owe a huge debt of gratitude to former Hockey Management Association officer, Malcolm McGaughy, (http://www.mcgdesign.net/), for the awesome logo design and other graphics in the book. A big thanks to Dan Myers, owner of Lazerpro Digital Media Group, and publisher of the websites StateCollege.com and OnwardState.com and his editor Geoff Rushton. They have given me a platform to develop my writing and storytelling skills.

Words cannot describe the gratitude I have for Terry and Kim Pegula and their family. They made a lifelong dream come true for this dreamer.

So many people in my life have contributed to all that went into creating Pragmatic Passion and inspiring me to put my thoughts and experiences in writing. So with "The Attitude of Gratitude" I want to thank:

Ken & Jamie B., John Bacon, Scott Balboni, Dr. Rod Bartell, Lt. Colonel Dick Bartolomea, Angie and Joe Battista, Coach Jan Battista, Sam Bernstine, Keith Blasé, Don Boller, Kate Booth, Rick Brandt, Rod Burnham, Paul and Karen Cervellero, Coach Al Clark, Dr. Paul Cohen, Tim Curley, John Davis, Janet DeBlasio, John DeBlasio, Dan Delligatti, Dr. Jason Engerman, Mr. Paul Fatur, Larry Fies, Coach Bob Ford, Bill Fustos, Gary Garrison, Scott Good, John Gray, Dean J.D. Hammond, Jeffrey Hayzlett, Dr. Dennis Heitzman, Bob and Mary Hershey, John Hook, Ruth Hussey, Norm Hutchison, Neen James, Coach Bob Johnson, Kyle Jordan, Al Karosas, Tom Keegan, Chuck Kensinger, Brad Killmeyer, Tim King, Rod Kirsch, Mr. Frank Kologie, Dr. Mark Konchar, Tom Kozlik, Dr. Morris Kurtz, Dan Leri, Dr. Ray Lombra, Bob Martin, Scott Martin, Joyce Matthews, Charles "Vance" McCullough, James McDuffie, Jim Meister, Steven Mezzacappa, Tammy Miller, Brad Mitchell, Dr. V.J. Nardy, Derek Nungesser, Dr. Nick Pappas, Ken Pasch, Mike Poorman, Lou Prato, Brian Price, David Reese, Loren Remetta, Larry Rocha, Dale Roth, Steve Sampsell, Herb Schmidt, Dr. Jack Selzer, Matt Seybert, Jon Shellington, Dr. Tom Sherwood, Scott Shirley, John Sieminski, Lynn Sipe, Paul Silvis, Steve Smith, Tyler Smith, Ken Snyder, Paul Steigerwald, David Stine, Dr. Andrew Strasser, Dean Jim Thomas, Laddie Thomas, Carolyn

Todd, Peter Tombros, Bill Waite, Tom Westfall, Dr. Billie Willits, Dr. David Wilson, and Jason Zivkovic.

A special thanks to my interns, Erica Salowe and Sam Borai, from the Donald P. Bellisario College of Communications at Penn State, for their hard work, great ideas, and patience. They both will go on to live joyful, fulfilling, and purposeful lives!

All have contributed directly or indirectly in some way to this book. There are so many others I wish I could thank in writing but that list could go on for quite awhile.

About the Author

[Photo Courtesy of Chuck Fong, Studio 2]

Joe Battista is a Professional Speaker, Success Coach, and Owner of Pragmatic Passion Consulting. He also serves as the Vice President of Business Development and an Executive Coach for the National Athletic and Professional Success Academy (NAPSA).

Joe has spent his entire career creating, building, growing, and transforming organizations and teams and serving "the greater good." He has been a coach and mentor for over a thousand coaches, colleagues, students, athletes, and campers. His passion for helping others is based on his long-time mantra that "someone has to care."

Joe has served in numerous capacities in business, intercollegiate athletics, and with professional sports teams including as Vice President of the Buffalo Sabres and Director of Amateur Hockey Development for the Pittsburgh Penguins. Joe spent 26 years at Penn State University (1987-2013) in roles including Associate Athletic Director; Executive Director of the Nittany Lion Club, and Head Coach of the Penn State Ice Hockey team that captured 6 American Collegiate Hockey Association (ACHA) National Championships and won 512 games in 19 years.

Battista helped secure the largest philanthropic gift in Penn State University's history, an $88 million donation through the generosity of Terry and Kim Pegula (owners of the Buffalo Bills and Buffalo Sabres). The gift grew to $102 million to build the Pegula Ice Arena and to establish two NCAA Division I ice hockey programs.

Joe is also recognized for his many contributions to growing interest in hockey in the United States, including 25 years as a USA Hockey Coaching Certification instructor. Joe was the head coach of Team USA for the 2003 World University Games. In 1991, he was a co-founder of the American Collegiate Hockey Association (ACHA), which has grown to a membership of almost 500 universities and colleges in five divisions. The ACHA has positively impacted thousands of male and female participants at the collegiate level.

In April of 2014, Battista received the prestigious "Lou Lamoriello Award" from the American Hockey Coaches Association for his distinguished professional career and contributions to the growth of hockey and has been inducted into The Penn Hills Sports Hall of Fame, The American Collegiate Hockey Association Hall of Fame, and The Pennsylvania Sports Hall of Fame.

A Pittsburgh, PA native, Battista is a 1983 graduate of Penn State University's Smeal College of Business with a degree in marketing. Joe and his wife, Heidi, (PSU class of 1981 B.S. and 1983 M.S.) live in State College and have a daughter, Brianna (PSU class of 2015) and two sons Jonathon (PSU class of 2016) and Ryan (a future Penn Stater), and their dog Barkley.

Citations

Introduction:

Gallup, Inc. "Gallup Daily: U.S. Employee Engagement." *Gallup.com*, news.gallup.com/poll/180404/gallup-daily-employee-engagement.aspx.

Hagel, John, and Alok Ranjan. "If You Love Them, Set Them Free." *Deloitte United States*, www2.deloitte.com/insights/us/en/topics/talent/future-workforce-engagement-in-the-workplace.html.

Gallup, Inc. "State of the American Workplace." Gallup.com, news.gallup.com/reports/199961/state-american-workplace-report-2017.aspx.

"Living Paycheck to Paycheck Is a Way of Life for Majority of U.S. Workers, According to New CareerBuilder Survey." *Press Room | Career Builder*, Career Builder, press.careerbuilder.com/2017-08-24-Living-Paycheck-to-Paycheck-is-a-Way-of-Life-for-Majority-of-U-S-Workers-According-to-New-CareerBuilder-Survey.

Huddleston, Cameron. "More Than Half of Americans Have Less Than $1,000 in Savings in 2017." GOBankingRates.com, 19 Sept. 2017, www.gobankingrates.com/saving-money/half-americans-less-savings-2017/.

Kirkham, Elyssa. "1 In 3 Americans Has No Retirement Savings | Money." *Time*, Time, 14 Mar. 2016, time.com/money/4258451/retirement-savings-survey/.

"Study: Nearly Half Of America's College Students Drop Out Before Receiving A Degree." *ThinkProgress*, ThinkProgress 28 Mar. 2012, thinkprogress.org/study-nearly-half-of-americas-college-students-drop-out-before-receiving-a-degree-68867634fa5e/.

US Census Bureau. "Highest Educational Levels Reached by Adults in the U.S. Since 1940." The United States Census Bureau, 30 Mar. 2017, www.census.gov/newsroom/press-releases/2017/cb17-51.html.

Kolet, Ilan. "College Tuition's 1,120 Percent Increase." *Bloomberg.com*, Bloomberg, 23 Aug. 2012, www.bloomberg.com/news/articles/2012-08-23/college-tuitions-1-120-percent-increase.

"Student Debt: Lives on Hold." *Consumer Reports*, 28 June 2016, www.consumerreports.org/student-loan-debt-crisis/lives-on-hold/.

Overture

Dachis, Adam. "'The Credit Belongs to the Man in the Arena.'" *Lifehacker*, Lifehacker.com, 15 Nov. 2013, lifehacker.com/the-credit-belongs-to-the-man-in-the-arena-1463520759.

Chapter 1

Cain, Susan. *Quiet: The Power of Introverts in a World That Can't Stop Talking.* Penguin Books, 2013

Chapter 2

Pascual, Jeanne San. "Why Attitude Is The Most Important Thing In Success." *Thought Catalog*, Thought Catalog, 18 Aug. 2017, thoughtcatalog.com/jeanne-san-pascual/2015/02/why-attitude-is-the-most-important-thing-in-success/.

Chapter 3

Neen, James. *Attention Pays.* Wiley, 2018.

"U.S. Life Expectancy Ranks 26th In The World, OECD Report Shows." *The Huffington Post*, TheHuffingtonPost.com, 21 Nov. 2013. https://www.huffingtonpost.com/2013/11/21/us-life-expectancy-oecd_n_4317367.html

The Empire Strikes Back. Directed by Irvin Kirshner. Performances by Mark Hamill, Harrison Ford, Carrie Fisher, Billy Dee Williams, Anthony Daniels, David Prowse, Kenny Baker, Peter Mayhew, and Frank Oz. Lucasfilm, 1980.

"Don't Confuse Movement With Progress - Denzel Washington Motivational Video." *YouTube*, YouTube, 26 Aug. 2017, www.youtube.com/watch?v=2V-TUs6m2oE.

"2014 Wasting Time at Work Survey" *Salary.com*, Salary.com, 2014. https://www.salary.com/2014-wasting-time-at-work/slide/2/

Lucier, Kelci Lynn. "The Top 10 Ways Students Waste Time in College." *ThoughtCo*, ThoughtCo, www.thoughtco.com/wasting-time-in-college-793171.

Chapter 4

Rimm, Allison. "Go Ahead: Ask Your Employees If They're Happy." *Harvard Business Review*, 7 Aug. 2014, hbr.org/2013/09/go-ahead-ask-your-employees-if-theyre-happy.

Chapter 5

Orndorf, Robert and Dulin Clark. *The PITA Principle: How to Work With and Avoid Becoming a Pain In The Ass.* JIST Pub., 2009

Chapter 6

McKay, Kate and Brett McKay. "The Eisenhower Decision Matrix: How to Distinguish Between Urgent and Important Tasks." *The Art of Manliness*, 27 May 2018, https://www.artofmanliness.com/2013/10/23/eisenhower-decision-matrix/

"Why the Analytics vs. Intuition Debate Misses the Mark." *DATAVERSITY*, 27 July 2015, www.dataversity.net/analytics-intuition-debate/.

bSci21. "9 Tips to Avoid Paralysis by Analysis." *Behavioral Science in the 21st Century*, 13 Nov. 2015, http://www.bsci21.org/9-tips-to-avoid-paralysis-by-analysis/

Chapter 7

Peters, Thomas. *In Search of Excellence*. Harper Business, 2006

Miller, M. Rex, et al. *Humanizing the Education Machine: How to Create Schools That Turn Disengaged Kids into Inspired Learners*. John Wiley & Sons, Inc., 2017.

Wijman, Tom. "Global Games Market Revenues 2018 | Per Region & Segment." Newzoo, 30 Apr. 2018, newzoo.com/insights/articles/global-games-market-reaches-137-9-billion-in-2018-mobile-games-take-half/.

Chapter 8

Jones, Ben. "State College, PA - Penn State Hockey: Nittany Lions Home Sell Out Streak Could Reach 57 This Weekend." StateCollege.com, 1 Mar. 2017,

"Penn State Only School with Two Venues Ranked among Top 100 Stadium Experiences." Penn State University, ConsumerAffairs, 25 Jan. 2018, news.psu.edu/story/502534/2018/01/25/athletics/penn-state-only-school-two-venues-ranked-among-top-100-stadium.

Made in the USA
Middletown, DE
08 January 2019